GW01458836

JOHN PIPER

JOHN PIPER

Anthony West

Secker & Warburg · London

First published in England 1979 by
Martin Secker & Warburg Limited
54 Poland Street, London W1V 3DF

Text Copyright © Anthony West 1979
Illustrations Copyright © John Piper 1979

SBN: 436 56590 0

Printed and bound in Great Britain
by W & J Mackay Limited, Chatham

Contents

Acknowledgments

The publisher, author and artist wish to thank the following for their kind permission to reproduce works:

Her Majesty Queen Elizabeth The Queen Mother

Her Royal Highness The Princess Margaret, Countess of Snowdon

Sir Colin Anderson; Bedford Art Gallery; James Cleveland Belle Esq; Bedford Art Gallery; Bristol Art Gallery; Sir Derrick Carter; Lord Clark; Hon Alan Clark MP; Villiers David Esq; Lady d'Avigdor-Goldsmid; Hirshhorn Collection, Smithsonian Institution, Washington DC; Patrick Horsbrugh Esq; Imperial War Museum, London; Leicester Galleries; Commander A. R. Mcdougall; Manchester City Art Galleries; Stanley Marcus Esq; Marlborough Fine Art; The Revd Dr W. M. Merchant; W. S. Mitchell Esq; Museum of Modern Art, New York; Sir Peter Pears; Phillips Memorial Gallery, Washington DC; Lord Rayne; Scottish National Gallery of Modern Art, Edinburgh; Sir Evelyn Shuckburgh; Reresby Sitwell Esq; Reynolds Stone Esq; Tate Gallery, London; Anthony Twentyman Esq; Vatican Gallery of Modern Art, Rome; Victoria & Albert Museum, London; Glynn Vivian Art Gallery, Swansea; Welsh National Museum, Cardiff; The Duchess of Westminster.

I

Although Alresford House, the mid-Victorian villa in Epsom in which John Piper was born, was torn down in 1910, when he was seven years old, its image remains so sharply defined in his memory that he can still, with his seventieth birthday behind him, draw it with as much certainty as if he had seen it yesterday. It was, as he remembers it, a pleasant, roomy house in the Italianate-Classical style of the late 1860s, built of yellowish stock brick with a white stucco trim. It stays in his mind as a house that he was fond of. But he does not offer to draw, or even to describe very precisely, the neo-Georgian building that his father put up in its place. He is content to say of this second Alresford that it was comfortable, and that it was built of very red brick. He does not dwell on the matter, and it seems clear that he never warmed to the new house—perhaps because he associated it with something, possibly an aspect of his father's approach to life, with which he felt at odds.

Not that they did not get on; indeed, over the long haul it may be said that they got on rather well, the father and son relationship being what it is. None the less there was a time, just after the ending of the First World War, when a strong divergence of views brought them to a rather painful confrontation. Piper had finished with Epsom College (where he had been a dayboy because his father had a humane objection to boarding-schools), and he wanted to go on to an art school to prepare himself for his chosen career as a painter. His father would not hear of it. Charles Alfred Piper, whose wife had given him three boys, had been very hard hit by the death of the oldest of them, Charles, in the second battle of Ypres in 1915. His thinking had thereafter been tinged by a profound pessimism. He was still taking a very dark view of what might lie ahead for England in particular, and for civilisation in general, when the question of his son's career came up in 1921. It was quite clear to him—the sort of drawings and paintings that his son was beginning to admire were proof enough of that, if proof were needed—that the visual arts were falling into the same state of confusion and anarchy as everything else. However things might have been in the past, when the Royal Academy was functioning as the firm centre of a rational art world, he could not feel that, with circumstances as they were, painting was still a profession. As all standards of excellence had gone by the board, there was no way of determining what goals its practioners should be attempting to achieve, and no way of predicting what might be expected as a reward for achieving them. In his view the profession had become a wildly chancy trade, with the odds weighted in favour of charlatans and stunt men. It was much too precarious to be relied upon as a man's sole resource. He insisted that his son should put the idea of embarking on a career as a painter right out of his mind until he had served his time as an articled clerk in a solicitor's office and qualified for practice as a principal. He was himself a solicitor, in business as the senior partner in his own law firm. His son would serve out his time in its offices at 13 Vincent Square in Westminster, with the virtual certainty of ultimately becoming a partner in the firm as an incentive to hard work. He would go on living at home meanwhile, the better to understand the benefits that hard work in a secure profession could bring—something he might not have appreciated while taking his home for granted as a child.

There was a great deal to be said for the good life of the Edwardian suburb as it was lived at Alresford. The house stood "in its own grounds" of about an acre, the last in a row of five such properties strung out along one side of what was to remain substantially a country lane until late in the 1920s. The family's cream, milk, butter, and eggs came from an entirely genuine farm across the way on an estate owned by Lord Rosebery; and beyond the Pipers' house the lane ran on between open fields to the wider freedoms of the Surrey Downs. Country sights and sounds were still very much a part of the local scene. The pleasure of starting out for school, or bicycling off on summer mornings to go exploring, between banks white with dead nettle and cow parsley, and blackbird-haunted hawthorn and blackthorn hedges have a high place in Piper's memories of his childhood. But it seems likely that his father thought that he would learn, as an office worker in Vincent Square, the value of the more practical advantages and less poetic satisfactions that he would have been blind to earlier in life.

There were the frequent trains offered by the two fiercely competing railways—the old London and South Western, and the London, Brighton, and South Coast—that took one to town and the office in twenty minutes, more or less, whenever one wanted; there was the help: the rooms in Alresford were swept and dusted, the beds made, and the

10

meals, cooked by the cook, were served, cleared, and washed up by the maids; there were winter flowers, and early tomatoes and cucumbers, brought in from the greenhouse by the gardener, who later on produced quantities of strawberries and soft fruit from under the tarred nets in the vegetable garden; and there was tennis on the tennis-court, and billiards on the full-sized table in the billiard-room . . . It was an ample, easy, and pleasant existence, and the father was sure that his son would come round to it, given time. He would be bound to see that it just was not common sense for a man to turn his back on the certain means of securing so much that was so good in order to have a gamble on his talent.

Charles Piper was in a position to enforce his will in the matter of his son's professional training, not so much because he held the purse strings, though he was ready to use that sanction, but rather because he held the trump card of his grievous loss. He did not consciously play it, and probably was not even aware that it was in the hand he was playing—but he did not have to be, it played itself. Piper was very fond of his father, and had no wish to add to the sadness and disappointment that his brother's death had brought to him by defying him. So he made no heroic gesture for the sake of his art, and through the winter of 1921, through 1922, through 1923, through 1924, and into 1925—although he was sure that he was sooner or later going to be a painter, and that he had to be, that he could not, in the end, possibly follow any other course—he went up from his father's house in Epsom on every working morning to spend the day in his father's offices in Vincent Square, learning how to search titles, and to draw conveyances and mortgage deeds.

Characteristically Piper has very little to say of this period of his enforced drudgery. He leaves much that might be said unsaid, and contents himself with the observation that his tutor in the office—his brother Gordon, who had been through the hoop three years ahead of him, and who was well set on the path that was to make him a partner, and later head of the firm of Piper, Smith, and Piper—was very patient with him. He prefers to speak of the gift of a tour of Northern Italy that his father gave to him in 1921, after he left school and before he went into the office. The trip was a family affair, and the little party of father, mother, and son set out in September of that year, to follow a route determined on beforehand, after a thorough study of Joseph Pennell's *On the Road in Tuscany*, that took them to Venice, Siena, Volterra, and San Gimignano.

Piper says that he will be eternally grateful to his father for having given him this glimpse of an Italy that was still very much as Ruskin and the dilettanti knew it, and still largely unaffected by ferro-concrete, tourism, and the motor-car, and his first sight of so much that has proved increasingly precious to him. It is possible, however, to see this expedition in another light, as a part of Charles Piper's effort to persuade his son to accept his professional fate as a solicitor. He was at pains to establish in the autobiography, guilelessly entitled *Sixty-Three: Not Out*, which he published in 1925, that he was, as John Rothenstein has put it, "a visual man with wide-ranging interests", and he may well have been doing his best to give his son proof in this way that one did not have to say good-bye to the world of art when one took up a profession. He, after all, had never given up his interest in drawing and watercolour-painting, although he had put it aside for a time while establishing himself in his business. But once he had felt solid ground under his feet he had put aside some of his leisure time to attend art classes at St Mary's School in Vincent Square, and he had subsequently derived a great deal of pleasure from his hobby—of making water-colour copies of pictures that he liked. In his time he was to produce a great many of these copies: the majority of them were of Turners, but there were also a considerable number of reproductions of works by the more advanced exhibitors at the Royal Academy's summer exhibitions, such as MacWhirter. This particular painter meant a great deal to him, and when he failed to secure his *June in the Austrian Tyrol*—it had been earmarked for the Tate Gallery—when it was first shown at the Academy he engaged a professional copyist to reproduce it for him. He was luckier with another Academy success, P. Marcius Simon's *A View of Florence*, and in that case managed to secure the original painting. Piper remembers the picture as telling very well against the dark blue canvas with which his father, rather dashingly for the date, had covered the walls of the Alresford dining-room in order to set it off.

The conclusion is inescapable, for the outsider at any rate, that the Italian expedition of 1921 was the well-intentioned offer, by a man with a very limited apprehension of what painting was all about, of half a loaf—a thing which may be better than no bread for the average hungry man with an average appetite to satisfy, but which can be no use at all to the dedicated artist. But, in any case, the plan misfired. Piper's father was taken ill in Siena, and was bedfast for a week in which his son was on his own in the town. He spent his time drawing, and his conviction bit deeper than ever. As soon as they were back in England

Piper told his father that he was serious, and that it was a vocation that was in question, not an interest that could be satisfied by indulgence in a part-time hobby, but he did not succeed in making his point. The best that his father would agree to would be a compromise: he was to be free to follow his chosen career, if he still wanted to, after he had passed the Law Society's examinations.

Coercive agreements of this kind, made when one party has the whip hand over the other, rarely work out well, and this one proved to be no exception to the general rule: Piper, although he had kept to his side of the bargain, had been working against the grain of his being from the moment he entered the office, and when the time came for him to take the final examinations he was not given a passing mark. His father died a year later, in 1926, before the stresses that this failure had generated between them had been fully resolved. It was in this somewhat desolating fashion that Piper was set free, at the age of twenty-three, to prepare himself for his chosen career.

The sequence of experiences that lead an artist step by step to the point at which he must recognise that he has no alternative but a commitment to his art is never particularly easy for him to describe, or for another to reconstruct. It has been suggested that Piper was especially fortunate in his early environment, which is said to have prepared him well for the pursuit of his vocation. In her brief but acute critical biography of Emily Brontë, Muriel Spark has a passage in which she discusses the remarkable way in which accounts of the childhood and youth of creative artists become polluted by knowledge of their later achievements. This factor seems to be at work here. Piper's subsequent mastery of the art of romantic landscape may be seen leaking back into the following statement in a recent biographical sketch: "His birthplace was 'Alresford', a villa in Ashley Road, Epsom, Surrey, named after the town in Hampshire where the Piper family had lived for several generations." So, indeed, they had, but several generations back. When Piper was born his parents had only lately moved out of town and into suburbia. They had lived until the previous year in the upper part over the Vincent Square offices in which Charles Alfred Piper carried on his business, in a district in which the family had well-established roots. The Vincent Square offices of Piper, Smith and Piper are about half a mile from the house in Bessborough Gardens, at the northern end of the Vauxhall Bridge, in which Charles Alfred Piper was born. That house had been bought by Charles Alfred's father when he moved out of the premises in the Horseferry Road, about a mile away to the east, in which he had been carrying on the bootmaker's business that had been started at the same address by *his* father, Charles Christmas Piper.

So far as John Piper can be said to have an organic connection with any particular piece of English soil it would appear to be with Ashley Road, Epsom, and with the London boroughs of Pimlico and Westminster. He had no regional connections through his mother, who was born Mary Ellen Mathews. Her father, who was of English origin, had spent most of his working life in and around the more solidly established racing-stables, while her Scotch mother had belonged to the superior class of indoor servant. Mrs Mathews had been housekeeper to the Duchess of Roxburghe at Haddington, and her elder daughter had been dresser to Queen Victoria's daughter, the Princess Beatrice. (While he was growing up Piper often went to have tea with his aunt in the grace and favour apartment in Kensington Palace which she occupied after her retirement.) Mary Ellen Mathews had, however, broken away from the family tradition of service, and by the time she became acquainted with Charles Piper she had established herself as a working partner in a smart hat-shop in Stratton Street, Piccadilly.

It will be seen that Piper's roots are less in a particular locality than they are in the solid middle ground of English life which produces thousands of men from Porlock for every one of its Coleridges. His early environment seems to have been no more and no less favourable to the development of an artist than one might infer from the fact that his second name—his full name is John Egerton Christmas Piper—was given to him as an act of homage to Thackeray. The environmental pressures that bore on him at the beginning of his life would have made him into a professional man who did a little sketching as a side line. It was something in him that made him resist them, and which led him on to become one of the most distinguished artists of his generation and one of the major figures in the history of the modern movement in English painting.

The temptation, all the greater since it is quite easy to do, for anyone writing a critical biography of Piper, is to fabricate an evolutionary account of the development of his interest in painting from the starting point offered by an anecdote of his early childhood in which he was described as being bowled over by the gift of a packet of postcards of the Turners in the Tate Gallery. These were given to him by his father as a reward for being brave at the dentist's. The Tate Gallery is just around the corner from Piper, Smith and Piper's offices in Vincent

Square, and the suggestion is that Piper began to be a regular frequenter of the Tate not too long after he received this reward. The theory has it that he in some sort absorbed painting into his bloodstream by so doing. This tale seems to be an enlargement on the fact that the father did, sometimes, when he had the boy on his hands for an hour or two before he was ready to take the train home to Epsom, turn the son loose in the Tate to amuse himself until he was through at the office. In reality Piper does not appear to have made significant use of the Tate until he had already become interested in painting and was in his last years at school. He cannot be said to have frequented the Gallery until later than that, when he was working in Vincent Square and could get to it in his lunch hours.

At the outset, until he was into his sixteenth year, he was not that interested in drawing or painting. He began drawing as a subsidiary activity to an interest in railways. In childhood he made a good many careful copies of photographs, line drawings, and coloured pictures of various kinds, illustrations of the engines and rolling stock of a variety of British and foreign railways. No examples of this work survive, and on the strength of his memories of it Piper says that this interest never took him beyond the most arid and unproductive kind of literal imitation. A sense that drawing might involve more than that first began to creep upon him after this initial interest had decayed in favour of another, in what might be called architectural antiquarianism. An uncle by marriage, Willie Harrison, persuaded him to share in an enthusiasm for the architectural monuments of pre-Renaissance English culture, and for the literature of the subject: the Batsford handbooks on church architecture and church fittings by such writers as Francis Bond and Charles Cox, and guidebooks written by people deeply infected by that enthusiasm for just such readers as Piper and his uncle—Methuen's Little Guides, and the regional and county guides in the Highways and Byways series.

Piper found in these guidebooks an absorbing interest, and when he was in his twelfth year, just as he was learning to use a camera and to develop his own films, he began to play an elaborate game in which he wrote and illustrated his own guides. These productions, pasted up in big, old-fashioned books, with leather-hinged board covers and marbled endpapers, of the kind that used to be sold in every properly conducted stationer's shop, were modelled on the volumes in the Highways and Byways series. They consequently had to be illustrated with line drawings. The earlier volumes in the series had been illustrated by Joseph

15

1 From a topographical notebook of 1921

Pennell and the later ones by F. L. Griggs. Both men had genuine gifts, but it would not be unfair to either to say that neither had given the job consistently of his best. For both of them what had initially been a labour of love had become an onerous piece of hackwork, and as Piper was producing his earliest guides he was, without knowing it, learning to use all the tricks and dodges that these two artists had devised to save themselves hard work during their years of servitude to the series.

The consequences of his becoming an accomplished, if unwitting, parodist of Pennell and Griggs were, however, unexpected. Part of his guidebook game was gathering material, and as he played it Piper spent more and more of his free time cycling through Surrey, Kent, Sussex, and the more immediately accessible parts of Hampshire, taking rubbings of memorial brasses, and photographing such things as lych gates, churches, and the more ancient farm houses. His photographs often overlapped the illustrations in the volumes in the Highways and Byways series, and Piper quickly came to see that Pennell and Griggs had

16

ROLLRIGHT STONES

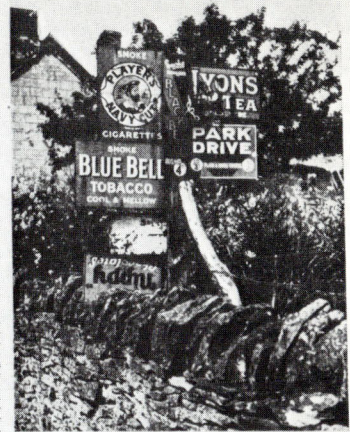

ROLLRIGHT

prehistoric stone circle, after Stonehenge and Avebury the most celebrated in England. Date uncertain, but very likely of the middle Bronze Age (that is, about 1500 B.C.). Circle is intriguing rather than impressive at first sight, because there are now three concentric circles; one of stones, one of fir trees and one of iron railings. But it is a place to go back to. The eighteenth-century antiquary-genius, Stukeley, who first put about stories of Druids and sacrifices that everybody took to (wrongly, modern archaeologists say), was very right in saying that the stones are "corroded like worm-eaten wood by the harsh jaws of time". *The King's Stone* is a monolith a hundred yards or so away (with its own private railings), of unknown use. *The Whispering Knights* (reasons for these names to be found in legends related locally, and in any other guide book) is a collection of stones a quarter of a mile away in a field—a dolmen, remains of a long-barrow. (These used to be called cromlechs). *Great Rollright* village is a grey, gawky place, but attractive. Roses, in season. There is an excellent cryptic, abstract carving (Romanesque) over a door in the church. Handsome tower and carved screen. *Little Rollright* is in a dip below the Stones: small and deserted—trees, a ruined barn, a church (for tomb-seekers), a manor house and a couple of cottages.

Rotherfield Greys and Rotherfield Peppard: 15: In the Henley-Reading corner of the county. *Peppard* has a common. *Greys* has a Court with ruins and towers, and old stables. Knollys and Stapleton monuments in the church.

Rousham: 8: Horace Walpole complimented the architect Kent on his alterations to the Rousham mansion. He liked the nice nonsense of Kent's new wings, and stables, and the temples and gates and sculptured wrestlers, and the sham castle over a mile away on a hill, that makes a living Claude. The church is rich in Jacobean pews. Also monuments and glass, and coats-of-arms on panels that might have been painted by Fernand Léger, the cubist: gay and angular.

Rycote: 12: In private Rycote Park is a chapel, charming in itself; rare in its contents. It

has wonderful woodwork, Renaissance and Jacobean: box pews, gay royal family pews (one on each side), stalls, reredos, altar rails, pulpit, gallery, powder-blue ceiling with gold stars: complete and unspoilt. Inside it suggests, somehow, a sailing ship under full sail in a light breeze. Rycote House was old, was burnt out, and has been olde-fied again.

Salford: 4: Doors and porches here are painted rich and subtle colours. Thomson of "The Seasons" might have been describing the country here when he wrote: "The landskip such, inspiring perfect ease". Round at the back of the church is a relief-carving (twelfth century) of

Sagittarius shooting his usual beast. **Sandford St. Martin:** 5: has less than half the population it had a hundred years ago. It is a good example of the rural village that has provided no substitute for the old arts and crafts, so it is neither developed nor arty. It has eighteenth-century houses and well built stone cottages. Ledwell, nearby, has even more the air of a deserted village. It is a place of old stone walls and bedraggled farmyards, and it has a manor site with enormous decrepit elm trees. **Sandford-on-Thames:** 11: A lock with a mill and an inn, downstream from Oxford on the Thames.

A Tree of Knowledge at SALFORD.

31

2 From the *Shell Guide to Oxfordshire*, by John Piper, 1938

frequently been guilty of substantial misrepresentations of their subjects. His first impulse was to substitute his photographs for drawings in his guides, but when he put his sepia prints beside his drawings on the page he discovered that the photographs were as unsatisfactory as the drawings. This disillusionment made him think about the techniques of drawing and photography as he had not until that time. He soon came to see that the formulae that he had picked up from his two partially discredited models were bound by their nature to lead to misrepresentations, and, perhaps more importantly, that some of the drawings that the two men had done for the series were very much better than the others. It was not, simply, that in some instances their drawings were more "like" the things represented, but that there was something in their treatment of a subject that gave looking at a particular drawing an especially close relationship to the experience of seeing the thing and being faced with it.

This perception, if it did not then express itself to him in the language

17

of art criticism, did take him to the art classes at Epsom College with the intention of learning how to make his drawings "come out" as he wished them to, and brought a new concern with seeing and looking into his cycling trips in search of antiquities. His discovery of the importance of vision led him to question the nature of the information that was of value to him. He had initially accepted unquestioningly the values of the past-oriented models offered to him by his uncle, and had seen little to argue with in the discursive obscurantism of the Highways and Byways series—which indoctrinated its readers with the thesis that nothing had gone well with the English arts of architecture, sculpture, and painting, since Henry VIII had put down the old religion and brought his Italian masons and craftsmen into the country. He had been just as uncritical about the antiquarian fanaticism of the Little Guides—whose editors were liable to dismiss any monument, civil or religious, of a later date than 1714 as "modern" and of no interest. But once he had become aware that there was something fundamentally wrong with the modes that he was using to give his knowledge of places and things graphic expression he became conscious of the extent to which his written texts were careful listings of what was irrelevant to the given experience.

The inner disquiet that his guidebook game generated within him slowly transformed the game into a genuine quest, both for a knowledge and understanding of the essences contributory to the sense of place, and for satisfactory modes through which that knowledge and understanding might be given expression. The seriousness of his commitment to this research led him on the one hand to adopt a scrupulous and methodical approach to the gathering of information which made him local secretary to the Surrey Archaeological Society when he was still in his sixteenth year, and on the other to form a determination to find some way of feeding the meaning of the information he was acquiring into the sketches that he was doing *sur place* in steadily increasing numbers.

This last determination brought Piper his first view of the arts from a standpoint other than that offered by his home and family background. Soon after he had outgrown the Dame School a short distance from Alresford, where his education had begun, and become a pupil at Epsom College, he made friends with Frank Milward, a boy of his own age who shared his interests and also did a little sketching. Milward pedalled along beside him on his antiquarian cycling expeditions, and as the sketching became an increasingly important part of the proceedings the two boys reached the conclusion that the watercolour paintboxes and the sketching-pads they were using were not the tools with which real artists got their results. The art master at Epsom College told them what materials to ask for, and gave them the name of the stationer's in the town where they would be able to find what they needed. This brought them into contact with the stationer's son, William Henry Birch, a keen young autodidact who was then working hard to develop the professional skills that were later to make him head of the Epsom Art School and a regular exhibitor at Burlington House. When David Birch, as he preferred to call himself, discovered the seriousness of Piper's interest in the problems of illustration he felt that his new acquaintance would benefit from a wider knowledge of the graphic arts in general than his antiquarian interest had given him. He accordingly suggested that, the better to keep abreast of what was going on in the field, they should pool their resources and take out joint subscriptions to *The Studio* and *Colour*.

Piper found *The Studio* of those years only negatively rewarding. The magazine was then running Sir William Orpen as the great reconciler. Its editor felt that his work had established a mode which would make it possible for those who wished to stay with the healthy and un-sensational English tradition of painting to do so without cutting themselves off from the main line of European painting. Orpen's masterwork —*The Studio*'s ideal painting at that time—was his self-consciously titled *Homage to Manet*, a picture which, not uninterestingly, shows that great confuser of issues, George Moore, in the act of reading what is presumably some kind of neo-Impressionist manifesto to Wilson Steer, Sir Hugh Lane, and Tonks, in the watchful presence of D. S. MacColl and Walter Sickert. The persons in the picture, however, played entirely sub-ordinate rôles, they were upstaged by three independent motifs: a pastiche of Manet's portrait of Eva Gonzalez which dominates its upper half, the portrait of a set of tea things on a table which fills in the space between Moore and his auditors, and the *trompe l'oeil* representation of a pair of gloves lying inside a top hat which calls for a degree of attention to which it has no logical or aesthetic claim from its bottom right-hand corner.

This show piece, apparently designed to prove that anything Frans Hals, Velazquez, Manet, and John Singer Sargent had done could be done again, struck Piper as typical of the sort of painting that the Tate was buying, under the Chantrey Bequest, out of the Academy—the subject picture whose purely arbitrary subject indicated only that the painter had an elaborate technique and no idea of what should be done with it. Discussing his failure to respond to this kind of work with Birch, who was inclined to be interested in displays of technique as such, Piper took his first conscious steps towards an interest in painting itself. He felt that there was something wrong, or at any rate inadequate and ill considered, in the use of colour in the typical *Studio* picture. Birch challenged him to say what that was, and Piper found himself at a loss until it occurred to him to compare the low return produced by the free use of colour by the academic subject painters with the rich effects achieved by the mediaeval stained-glass designers making disciplined use of a severely restricted range of colours. Birch objected that Piper was confusing one medium with another, but he did not feel able to accept that. He began looking with sharpened attention at the stained glass in the churches he visited, and at the rather different sort of painting that *Colour* was showing him.

What *Colour*, as opposed to *The Studio*, stood for is best indicated by quoting the names of the artists whose work was represented in the show with the general title of The New Movement in Art which opened in Heal's Mansard Gallery in October 1917. The painters concerned were Boris Anrep, George Barnes, Vanessa Bell, Brancusi, Gaudier-Brzeska, Dolores Courtney, André Derain, Henri Doucet, Frederick Etchells, Othon Friesz, Roger Fry, Mark Gertler, Duncan Grant, Juan Gris, Maria Guitherrez, Nina Hamnett, E. McKnight Kauffer, Roald Kristian, André Lhote, Jean Marchand, G. Thiesson, and Vlaminck.

The name on this list then considered by many, chief among them Roger Fry, to be the big one, and the best bet as far as indicating the future direction of painting was concerned, was that of Marchand. Birch took Marchand seriously (and Marchand turned out to be known to John Hilton, a younger friend of Piper's father, who owned some examples of his work, among them the then much reproduced *L'Avenue*) so Piper did his best to do the same. A small monograph devoted to Marchand's work was, indeed, one of the first art books he purchased on his own account, but he was never able to achieve a genuine enthusiasm. Marchand's drawings, not unlike those being done at the time by Augustus John, carried some degree of conviction for him, but the paintings did not. Piper saw that there was an affinity between Marchand's painting and Roger Fry's — it rather rapidly became clear to him that Fry, whether he knew it or not, was painting in the manner of Marchand—but it was also plain to him that there was some

3 The stoning of St Stephen: 13th-century stained glass panel at Grateley, Hampshire. One of the first of a continuing series of actual-size copies, 1929

essential difference between what the painter was doing, and what Fry was attempting to do, that was unlike what most of the other painters presented in *Colour* were doing, particularly those who were working in France.

A suspicion entered his mind that Marchand and Fry were concerned with a false modernism, like that of Orpen and *The Studio*, involving a repetition of what had been done by Cézanne in place of a repetition of what had been done by Manet — and so more acceptable to the extent that Cézanne had been the more interesting painter, for painters anyway, but only to that extent. The more promising men proposed by *Colour* as significant contributors to the modern movement seemed to be engaged in another kind of exercise. They were not looking back towards Cézanne's accomplished work, but looking on from it. This suspicion could not be taken further than that at that stage in Piper's development, partly because he had no terminology in which to make the necessary formulations, and partly, and more influentially, because he did not have the necessary visual experience of painting to do so. His suspicion then had to stop at the intuition that there was something stale in the "feel" of the work produced by the Cézannists of Marchand's school that was not in Cézanne's own work.

Piper did not understand what Cézanne had been doing with paint and colour at this stage, but he was following his personal intuitive rather than cognitive route towards an understanding of it; at first sight a regressive one that involved concentrating his attention on what was being done by Frank Brangwyn, James Pryde, and Sir William Nicholson.

One of the lessons that artists have to teach art historians and theorists is that painters often learn their first and most valuable lessons from looking at work well below the level of their own subsequent achievements, Picasso's fascinated early tributes to the coarsely executed and coarsely imagined works of Forain being a case in point. Brangwyn's sensitivities, as a painter, were in a class with Forain's, and most readers who know his work at all will associate his name with a sort of holidays-in-the-sun exoticism, involving what can only be called vulgar treatments of tropical local colour. But this is to remember some late decorative work done for the House of Lords, and to forget the flower paintings that Brangwyn was doing before 1920: in these he was drawing with colour and using oil paint in such a way as to make its intrinsic qualities express the characteristics of flowers as flowers.

Looking at these paintings Piper first saw that there could be a use of paint and its qualities as interesting and as rich in possibility as the use of the qualities of glass by the stained-glass workers. The entering wedge of this intuition came from looking at the work of James Pryde and Sir William Nicholson — not at the paintings they did separately as individuals, but at the graphic work they did together as the Beggarstaff Brothers. The importance of this work as a breakaway from the

22

English tradition of linear draughtsmanship has only recently been given its proper critical recognition by James Thorpe, and by the German critic Dr Herta Wescher, who has dealt with it in her massive study of collage. It influenced Ben Nicholson's development by the simplest and most natural of processes, and worked on Piper's because he recognised, as soon as he asked himself why it appealed to him, that the characteristic Beggarstaff style was the function of a technique parallel with that used in the making of mediaeval stained-glass windows.

The parallel will not be obvious to those who think of the Beggarstaff style as very much of the 1890s and closely related to Beardsley's. It only becomes apparent when it is realised that the originals from which their posters were printed were collages. Pryde and Nicholson got their effects by ruthlessly simplifying their subjects until they were reduced to map-like schemes that could be rendered by two or three areas of strong colour placed in juxtaposition against a lighter monochrome background. They controlled their process by drawing outlines of the areas of strong colour onto sheets of appropriately coloured paper. These were then cut to the outline and pasted onto a white or colour-washed background sheet. An important element in their style that was extremely advanced in their day was that the boundaries of the colour areas were arbitrary and in themselves non-representational — in isolation they were signs without meaning, which they acquired by association with the adjacent areas. The layout was converted into a representational sign within the mind of the person looking at it. This is, of course, true to some extent of all representations of three-dimensional objects on plane surfaces, but in their commercial work Pryde and Nicholson made demands for collaboration of a kind that Western European painters had effectively given up making at the time of the great representational revolution of 1425–50. It is significant that they were designers of posters: public announcements that must catch the eye and rivet the attention in competition with the distracting visual arrays offered by streets and hoardings. They can only succeed if they appeal directly through the eye to the instinctive pre-cognitive and non-verbal mental processes—those that receive, store, and retrieve holograms without rationalisation or verbalisation.

Piper did not get this as a message from Pryde and Nicholson's work since they were not ideologues. Unlike Gauguin, who had used areas of colour in just the same way, and said what he was up to, they were putting their theories into practice without explaining them. It was, however, through their work that he had his initial glimpse of the possibility that there might be an entirely non-literary, non-verbal language of the eye that an artist might learn to use.

Piper had come this far when his two years of discovery, 1919 and 1920, broke his world wide open. These years brought him three explosively stimulating encounters, with the work of Picasso, Blake, and Rouault. In September of 1918 Diaghilev had brought the Russian Ballet to London to fill a limited engagement at the Alhambra Theatre in Leicester Square. Success transformed what was to have been a fleeting visit of a few weeks into a run of nearly a year, and when, towards the end of that period, Diaghilev added two new ballets to the company's repertory, the event proved to be one of the turning points in the history of English art.

The costumes and scenery Picasso had designed for the de Falla-Massine ballet *The Three-Cornered Hat*, and Derain's designs for *Boutique Fantasque*, came as a revelation of what the new movement in art was all about to the new generation—of which Piper was a junior member —which had come up during the War. The pointsman of the avant-garde in the English theatre before the war had been Gordon Craig, an anti-painter, whose drive had been for the liberation of the stage designer from a stage picture modelled on the contemporary academic subject picture, and second-wave support had been the garden-suburb modernism of Lovat Fraser. The bold calligraphic simplifications and the brilliant use of colour in *The Three-Cornered Hat* designs simultaneously provided a demonstration of a new idea of what a picture could be, and showed what that new pictorial idea could bring to the theatre.

With a great many other people of his age group Piper passed across the laconic bridge which was such a stunning feature of Picasso's great stage picture into the world of modern painting. *The Three-Cornered Hat* designs were wholly free of the characteristics which had made it possible to dismiss Picasso's *Parade* as an aberration and a stunt—they were at once a departure into a new domain and a contribution to the established tradition of stage design. Piper was enormously impressed by the authority and certainty with which Picasso's scheme for the ballet had been carried out, and his excitement at the discovery of a new master painter was made all the greater by the association of *The Three-Cornered Hat* with *Boutique Fantasque*. Derain's work was a lighter and less substantial effort, but it none the less showed that this new visual language was not one that would suppress individual voices.

24

That a new visual language was in question was an idea that presented itself to him when, in the middle of his excitement at his discovery of Picasso, he encountered Blake. Piper had been too young to wish to see the Tate's Blake exhibition of 1913, the first English show to put the poet to the public as a painter and graphic artist worth taking seriously. In the atmosphere in which he was brought up, the prevailing view of Blake's work, so far as there can be said to have been one, was that the paintings and drawings came from Blake's dotty side. The general reaction in March 1918 when Blake momentarily came into the news as an artist was a scandalised "Did you ever?" To pay £7,665 for a set of pictures by a man whose chief claim to fame was that he had drawn the ghost of a flea! And in wartime, too! That was just the sort of thing clever people, or people who called themselves clever, might be expected to do! The sum, rather than the pictures themselves, Blake's hundred and two illustrations to Dante's *Divine Comedy*, was what attracted attention: it had been raised by a consortium of institutions, the Tate Gallery, the British Museum, the City Art Gallery of Birmingham, the Ashmolean Museum in Oxford, the Truro Museum, the National Gallery of Victoria in Melbourne, and the Fogg Museum in Cambridge, Massachusetts. They had combined forces to defeat the Linnell family's attempt to dispose of them in such a way that they would not be dispersed. By way of making a partial atonement for what was being done, the complete set of illustrations was put on show in the Tate after the War had ended.

Piper had already seen the Blakes that had come from the National Gallery to the Tate in 1909, and those others acquired by the Gallery in that year and in 1914, but he had seen them unsupported by the knowledge of the whole range of this painter's work that is needed if his individual productions are to be properly understood. Looking at the Dante illustrations Piper saw for the first time Blake's productions as works of art rather than as curiosities and for the first time realised the importance of looking through a picture's stated content to the painter's performance, that is to say, to the painting as an action. He was especially struck by the extraordinary force and beauty of the calligraphic treatment of the vegetation in the drawings of *Dante and Virgil Penetrating the Forest*, and *The Inscription Over the Gate*. He was as greatly impressed, though in a slightly different way, by the no less powerful and beautiful solutions Blake had found for the problems presented by the distant views in the backgrounds of *The Laborious Passage Along the Rocks* and *The Pit of Disease*, and by the necessity for suggesting enormous voids between the foregrounds and the backgrounds in the two plates called *The Ascent of the Mountains of Purgatory* and *Dante and Virgil Approaching the Angel Who Guards the Entrance of Purgatory*. These two had an especial significance for him as they led him to an understanding of a third—*The Rock Sculptured with the Recovery of the Ark and the Annunciation*. This drawing is closely related to the other two in theme and composition, but thrillingly unlike them in that it makes its ostensible subject matter entirely secondary to the manner in which the pencil, pen, and watercolour drawing has been set down on the paper. The main subject, the thing the drawing may be said to be, finally, about, is the cascading line descending from its top right-hand to its bottom left-hand corner; this seizes the imagination by the dramatic way in which it divides the plain surface on which it has been laid into two balanced sections.

The excitement of his discovery that Blake the painter was capable of doing such a thing naturally led Piper to plunge into the works of Blake the writer—with the usual results, at once stimulating and confusing. Piper found himself carried straight to the heart of what the modern movement in painting is concerned with, and has been all along, by Blake's unforgettable question: "Shall painting be confined to the sordid drudgery of facsimile representations of merely mortal and perishing substances and not be, as poetry and music are, elevated to its own proper sphere of invention and visionary conception?" The question hit Piper with special force because he came on it just as his personal visual experience had brought him to the point at which he was ready to entertain the idea that painting might be, like music, a non-literary, non-descriptive art, concerned with making statements that were ends in themselves. He had just recognised that the power and effectiveness of mediaeval glass had come from its subordination of subject matter to colour relationships and the balance of colour masses, and had come to see that the art had decayed as it had become didactic and increasingly inclined to the use of colour simply to lend plausibility to illustrative line drawings placed on the surface of the glass without regard to its inherent qualities. The conclusion was inescapable, that stained glass had been good when it had drawn on its proper sphere of invention and spoken its own language, and that it had become debilitated with the use of an inappropriate vocabulary, drawn from another art.

The habit of using church glass as a reference point when thinking about pictures, and a certain alarmed fascination with the sensual and physical worlds that his own development was, naturally enough, bringing to his attention, took him on from Blake to Rouault. This was in 1920, when his growing interest in painting led him to buy the little book in the Gallimard series, *Les Peintres français nouveaux*, devoted to Rouault's work.

The story of Piper's copy of this book is about what growing up is like, and what he was at this time growing through and away from. He was seeing more and more of his father's friend John Hilton in these years. He had been on walking tours with him in his last two summer holidays while he was at Epsom College, and through 1919 and 1920 he was spending almost every weekend with him at his cottage near Beaconsfield.

Although it was near Beaconsfield, it was called The Dacha—because Hilton, on the pretext of taking care of his health, had made the liberal pilgrimage to Constance Garnett's Russia before the War. Hilton was that kind of person, a sweetly, wholly serious member of the old Clarion crowd who had come from Bolton in Lancashire, and was on his way through a career in the Ministry of Labour which was to end during the Second World War when he was at the Ministry of Information laying the propaganda foundations for an acceptance of the Beveridge report and the making of the Welfare State. He was a kind man with good intentions and, knowing that Piper's father despaired the decay of the English poetic tradition, sent him at about this time a copy of "Trees" to convince him that good poems were still being written.

Hilton had spotted Piper as a comer, and to widen his horizons had him over to The Dacha to meet his literary friends Richard Church and G. K. Chesterton. When his friend the painter Marchand came to England to stay with him, he brought him over to Alresford for Sunday lunch and an afternoon of croquet. Piper initially got on rather well with the great man. But this new acquaintanceship soured not long after.

Piper knew that the Rouault volume in the Gallimard series had just come out in France and, finding it unobtainable in England, asked Hilton, who was about to go on a visit to Paris, to do him the favour of having it sent to him. Hilton did not have time to execute the commission himself and, knowing that Piper had made a very favourable impression upon Marchand, asked him to have his bookseller do the job: he received a fierce turn-down in reply: Marchand certainly was not going to send Piper, or anyone else, a book about Rouault, who was pretty close to being a pornographer, and who could only be a pernicious influence on a green young man like Piper. And while Hilton was at it, he might tell his young friend to forget all about Picasso, who was not to be admired—Picasso was, if anything, an even bigger faker than Rouault—Hilton should warn young Piper to be very careful about what he looked at.

Hilton passed this on to Piper with his usual sweet seriousness—it was after all a serious warning from an experienced and accomplished man to an inexperienced beginner, it could save him from serious mistakes. Piper had to get his Rouault opuscule from another source, but that was not as important as the ending of Hilton as a serious influence, and the ending of any possibility of taking Marchand seriously as a painter— which meant an end to any thought of taking Roger Fry seriously as a critic, since he was an advocate of Marchand's seriousness. For good or ill the young make the important decisions that determine their futures in this way. When Piper got the Rouault book at last it was already invested with a special importance for him, and he was pre-disposed to accept the idea of a painting that emerged from Rouault's work. The traces left on it by Rouault's apprenticeship in Hirsch's stained-glass studio struck the chord of his interest in mediaeval church glass, and he was immediately responsive to its strongly dramatic character, as character which derives much more from the self-imposed limitation on the palette—black, dark blue, red, indian red, yellow—than from the subject matter.

Piper was also profoundly affected by the element in Rouault's painting that caused Leon Bloy such acute distress, the sombre violence of its sensuality. Celtic in its origin in Rouault, it touched something Celtic in his own make-up, the Indian something that is part of the Indo-European heritage, and which is most compactly stated by the personification of Kali as a goddess: the mother and the destroyer of all things. Just as the full effect of Rouault's experiences in Hirsch's studio only became manifest in his work after he had been through the Ecole des Beaux-Arts under Gustave Moreau, so the shock of a recognition of something within himself in Rouault's early nudes only made itself visible in Piper's work in the middle 1930s after an interval of just over a decade.

What was exciting to him at the time, and what he was fully conscious of, was the interest of the rich effects produced with the limited palette, and the painterly technique. But in the end, the importance to him of the discovery of Rouault was that it was, coming on top of the

28

discoveries of Picasso and Blake, the clincher. After he had made it there was no possible alternative to painting, he knew exactly what he was to do with his life, and what his life was to be *for*. But he was faced with the classic problem of the gifted adolescent who has been accorded such a revelation of aim and purpose, his insight was divorced from a mastery of the techniques needed to give his conviction justification. It was all very well to say, "I have to be a painter—I am a painter—an artist" but he could not provide the necessary proofs in the way of skill and manifestations of talent. And worst of all, he was still a schoolboy, and in adult eyes, more so then than now, a child. He could still be put down very easily with the old arguments—you don't know very much about these things, you don't know very much about the world, you still have a great deal of growing up to do.

And there was, to tell the truth, something in it: while mentally ready to take part in the liberation of painting from sordid drudgery, as Blake had defined it, Piper was still in 1919–20 just about ready to win the Epsom College Drawing Prize with some very standard art-room drawing. Blake had answered his own questions in his own way. "No! It shall not be so. Painting, as well as poetry and music, exists and exults in immortal thoughts." What Blake may have intended by the last two words in this sentence, or even a satisfactory interpretation of them, was only to be discerned by someone with a great deal of painting, or of growing up, behind him: whichever it was, Piper still had it to do.

A great many threads go into the weaving of a fine cloth, and the way they come together is sometimes odd. Piper's father was interested in music, but musically illiterate, a condition that made him a natural customer for the newly introduced player piano, and from as far back as Piper can remember, the Pianola he bought was part of the life of Alresford House. Now that the instrument has been superseded by electronic reproducers with a much wider range the idea of the player piano has become something of a camp joke, and the machine is thought of as a comic manifestation of Edwardian musical philistinism. It is forgotten that in its brief hour it was quite the best reproducer of piano-music that was going. Even a musically illiterate operator who followed the directions with reasonable care could duplicate the performance of the virtuoso whose performance had been cut onto the master roll with a very large degree of accuracy. A player-piano owner who had access to a good library of Pianola rolls could familiarise himself with the sound of a large part of the repertory of music written for the pianoforte. Charles Piper had been one of the original subscribers to the London Aeolian Company's lending library of Pianola rolls, and he encouraged his family to make use of it. Piper began pumping away at his father's machine just as soon as his legs grew long enough to allow him to reach the foot pedals, and as he worked away with his feet, and followed the waverings of the dotted tempo line with the brass manual control, he began to see that the different names on the rolls stood for different ways of doing different things. A vague and diffuse keenness for musical sounds was slowly transformed into a desire to understand what the composers had intended, and what they had done to fulfil their intentions, to become a musically literate and competent pianist who could make such sounds at will and know what he was doing.

That, rather simply at first, meant "music" as a school extra, but when Piper turned out to have a natural talent for the piano, it led to special lessons from James McKay Martin, the church organist at Fetcham near Leatherhead. Martin liked Piper for himself and for his enthusiasm for music, was supportive and encouraging, and introduced him to his friend Vaughan Williams. Piper liked and admired his teacher, and respected his taste and judgment, and so presently ran himself into the kind of trap that the world sets for the young and inexperienced.

The stimulation that he had been given by the Diaghilev ballets started him off on his own set and costume designs, and he began to make eager use of such opportunities as he was offered by the series of musical shows put on annually in the Epsom Congregational Hall by an amateur group under the direction of a certain Roger de Wesselow. When the initial exhilaration caused by seeing his own work on a lighted stage had worn off a little Piper began to be bothered by the low musical tone of the enterprise, and brought his friend James Martin into the group in the hope of bringing about an improvement in its standards. He did not foresee the violence with which de Wesselow would react to this implied criticism of his taste and competence, or the brutality with which he would appeal to the latent snobbery of a section of the group's membership in the defence of his little empire. Piper was made to feel the enormity of what he had done—he had questioned dear Mr de Wesselow's musical judgment, and offered him *advice* and *help*, as if a few lessons in piano-playing from the son of the Epsom sanitary inspector had made him some kind of expert! It was not as easy to shrug this off as it might have been, because James Martin did rather mind having been put into a position in which his father's line of work could be used against him—half of him could laugh at the absurdity of the tiny storm in the tiny teapot, but not the other half. And then, when it came to the point, Piper did not have the musical knowledge or the musicianship necessary to support the sort of challenge that he had inadvertently offered to de Wesselow.

He realised that he was in need of rather more than James Martin had in him to give if he was to establish his right to have his say in such matters. A solution to the problem of where it was to come from lay surprisingly close to hand. As rather half-hearted members of the Church of England, Piper's father and mother formed part of the congregation of their parish church, St Martin's, which had just taken on a new curate, a young man called Victor Edward Glencoe Kenna, who had gone into the Church on being demobilised from his wartime service with the Marines. Kenna was a gifted amateur pianist who had been a pupil and who had become a friend of Arthur Schnabel, and he now took over Piper's musical education, introducing him to the world of musical scholarship and discriminating criticism, and to the classical as opposed to the merely enthusiastic approach.

Kenna, a Cornishman by origin, was a good deal more than the sort of diffusely cultured young clergyman who was not uncommonly found sheltering from the harsher realities in Victorian and Edwardian rectories: he was a scholar with an acute and perceptive critical intelligence who was in due course to become an authority on the seals, intaglios, and coins of the prehistoric and classical periods in Greece and the Middle East. As Piper came to know him better he disclosed a wide range of interests, in architecture, in archaeology, in prehistoric art, and in contemporary painting. Kenna's background of serious scholarship added a new dimension to the amateurish antiquarianism into which Piper had been initiated by his uncle Willie. Kenna introduced him to the formalisations and abstractions characteristic of Celtic and Middle-Eastern prehistoric art, and through his archaeological knowledge opened for him the world of meanings that lay behind the sensuous appeal of the serene time-softened shapes of the great earth works, the hill-top forts, the barrows, and the old trackways and terracings under the close cropped downland turf of southern and southwestern England.

But, more importantly, Kenna had the knowledge of contemporary painters and painting that enabled him to call Piper to order in the matter of his emotional reaction against Hilton's conventional wisdom and Marchand, and his consequent rejection of Cézanne and the

Cézannists. Piper had told Kenna, among other things, that the impact upon him of the sheer authority of the work of Picasso and Rouault had carried him on beyond the point at which Cézanne's gropings could mean anything to him. Kenna was able to bring him back to a recognition of the way in which Picasso's vision had risen directly, and Rouault's by an only slightly less direct path, from Cézanne's methodical liquidation and reconstitution of forms by the use of colour.

This was part of a larger programme, in the nature of a rescue operation. Kenna had recognised Piper's potential and the extent to which it was endangered by provincialism, and he felt that it was an urgent matter to get him out of the small teapot in which he would be in danger of wasting his substance and psychic energy on confrontations with people like de Wesselow and, perhaps even more dangerously, on loose enthusiasms. He wanted to bring, so far as he could, his young friend within sight at any rate of the main stream, even if he could not toss him into it, and to give him a bracing sense of the importance of some kind of intellectual discipline.

Kenna was enlightened in the mode of the decade, and very much a member of the generation involved in the repudiation of what literary specialists in the period refer to as "the weekend". The reference is to a poem of Harold Monro's:

> *The Train! The Twelve O'Clock for Paradise*
> Hurry, or it will try to creep away.
>> Out in the country everyone is wise:
> We can only be wise on Saturday.
>> There you are waiting little friendly house,
> Those are your chimney stacks, with you between,
>> Surrounded by old trees and strolling cows,
> Starting through all your windows at the green.
>> Your homely floor is creaking for our tread;
> The smiling teapot with contented spout
>> Thinks of the boiling water, and the bread
> Longs for the butter. All their hands are out
>> To greet us, and the gentle blankets seem
> Purring and crooning: "Lie in us and dream."

This may have been only a joke, or a piece of affable condescension, but it did get itself on to page 82 of the third volume of *Georgian Poetry*, and at the time it epitomised the end-of-the-line bankruptcy which had overtaken the romantic impulse in poetry in general, and the particular parochialism and inadequacy of the brand of modernism of which the Georgian poets had been the fuglemen. It was appalling to the young men of Kenna's generation to find that "weekending" was to be resumed as soon as the revelatory nightmare of the 1914–19 War had come to an end. The post-War *Georgian Poetry*, Volume V, struck the pre-War vein again and again.

> And I will take celandine, nettle, and parsley, white
> In its own green light,
> Or milkwort and sorrel, thyme, harebell and meadowsweet
> Lifting at your feet
> And Ivy blossom beloved of soft bees; I will take
> The loveliest—
> The seeding grasses that bend with the winds, and shake
> Though the winds are at rest.
>
> John Freeman

Knowing that Piper had already found his way to Harold Monro's Poetry Bookshop on his own, Kenna was very much afraid of this, and what it stood for, as a more than likely end-product of the Highways and Byways romanticism that had been his route to an interest in the past, and the origins of the present. He had himself been responsive to the call for the hard, dry and sophisticated, formulated by T. E. Hulme and Richard Aldington on the eve of the War, and to the warning issued in the middle of it by T. S. Eliot, in the cause of a rejection of the inadequate philosophic basis for the romantic conception of nature— "the vague is a more dangerous path . . . than the arid." He recognised in Piper's interest in Blake's "immortal thoughts", Celtic longings for Conla's Well, the dark pool inhabited by the salmon of intuition in the shadow of a blasted oak and towering crag, the source of a dangerous weakness for the very things that those who were then defining the terms of the modern movement were at pains to condemn.

Kenna eased Piper into a region of more exacting standards than he had been used to—gently at first, by way of an excursion to Oxford to see some genuinely modern pictures, by men whose work he had until then only known in reproduction, in Michael Sadleir's collection. He introduced Piper to the anti-Georgian magazines and publications, such as *Wheels*, which published Osbert and Edith Sitwell, Aldous Huxley, and Herbert Read; *Arts and Letters*, which carried on, under the editorship of Frank Rutter, the work of *Wheels* with a broadened base that included Ezra Pound and T. S. Eliot; to the Oxford magazine *Coterie*, which published Tommy Earp, Wilfred Childe, Herbert Read, and Conrad Aiken; and in due course to Eliot's own *Criterion*. Kenna brought these manifestations of the spirit of the modern movement to Piper's attention for positive as well as negative reasons. It was not simply that he wanted to engage Piper in a complex of trendy repudiations—he wanted him to think out for himself why, for instance, as he saw it, T. E. Hulme had been right to take what he did from Wilhelm Worringer, and dead wrong to dilute what he got from that admirable source with what Ezra Pound had coarsely called "crap like Bergson".

This was getting back into 1913, the crisis year for the Vorticists, in which Hulme had come back from Berlin speaking in a new voice that made better sense than Wyndham Lewis' utterances. Hulme had gone off to Berlin at the end of 1912 as the translator of Bergson's *Introduction to Metaphysics*, and had returned as an ardent propagandist for Worringer who had been lecturing on Art that winter. Pound and Lewis were taken aback to find that the man they had almost written off as having no understanding of the arts was now saying almost exactly what they wanted to say.

The theory that had seized Hulme's fancy was that there were basically two kinds of human culture, each producing its appropriate types of art, the essential characteristics of which could be epitomised by the two words "abstraction" and "empathy". According to Worringer, abstraction in art is symptomatic of a culture that either fears or radically mistrusts nature, in the one case feeling an immense spiritual dread of space, and in the other that the visible world is an illusion. In either case the end-product of the attitude is the impossibility of a confident surrender to the outer world or the development of any form of individualism. What follows from the absence of these things is an art making few if any references to everyday realities, and characterised by highly stylised and non-representational forms divorced from signs and indicators pinning them to specific locations in time and space. Empathy was the characteristic of essentially scientific and rational cultures. These were unafraid of both the natural and the supernatural, and so capable of trusting life, and of developing the concept of individualism. The art of such a culture is likely to be rich in all the devices required for naturalistic representation of the visible world of common experience, chiaroscuro, modelling, foreshortening, and perspective, all of which are means to the end of representing the particular thing, in the given place, at the specific hour.

34

Worringer, who put his theory on paper in the first six years of the century, and had it published in 1908, the same year in which Meier-Graeffe's *Modern Art* came out, was the first critic to speak of the Renaissance as a period of lost creative options. He described it as the "great period of bourgeois naturalness" and said that "all unnaturalness—the hall-mark of all creation determined by the urge to abstraction—disappears . . ." as it begins. He goes on to say that "Whoever has felt, in some degree, all that is contained in this unnaturalness, despite his joy at the new felicity created by the Renaissance, will remain conscious with deep regret, of all the great values hallowed by an immense tradition that were lost forever with this victory of the organic, of the natural." The argument Worringer developed was the charter of modern eclecticism, the first formal academic repudiation of the absolute character of the standards of beauty established by Classical Greece and Renaissance Italy.

Hulme—who was at once very English and an intellectual thug, and consequently interested in abstract theories only in so far as they could be given practical application or used in a feud—took up Worringer's ideas as the perfect weapons with which to advance the Vorticist cause and to beat up Roger Fry and Clive Bell. Worringer liked Graeco-Roman and Renaissance art, and their derivatives, but Hulme wanted to clear away all that was soft, naturalistic, and pleasure-oriented. He held that it was "the duty of every honest man to clean the world of these sloppy dregs of the post-Renaissance". This was Hulme at his bully-boy worst, hot to clean the floor with the opposition, and sinking to any silliness for the sake of getting in a blow beneath the belt. He was a great deal less bumptious, and less objectionable, when it came to saying what he was for, however, carrying on Worringer's argument and asserting the value of the artifacts of alienation, a term by which he meant the sense of man's isolation from his physical environment, the works of art produced by the cultures of Africa, Byzantium, India, and Egypt.

But while Hulme was willing to make full use of the licence he had received from Worringer to find beauty in such conventionally "hideous" things as African masks, he was concerned to make the point that there was no point in shopping off one academism for another—nothing was to be gained by harking back to the achievements of primitive cultures as the academics had harked back to those of Classical Greece and the Renaissance. The contemporary artist was immersed in his own industrial and mechanical culture, the development of which had changed the character of human sensibility, and he could only function as an artist if he gave expression to its values. It was idle, the culture of industrial civilisation being what it was, to go on talking in terms of beauty, grace, harmony, rhythm, and balance; the new sensibility valued the austere, the clean-cut, the spare, the efficient—the qualities of metals worked by machine tools, and of the structures, and structural relationships characteristic of machinery and engineering projects. Hulme pointed out, with some acuteness, the triviality, and the essential vulgarity, of Marinetti's effort to get the artist into the business of doing pictures of machines: it was the artist's job to liberate mechanical forms from particular machines, and to discover images that would express dynamic relationships. He spoke highly of Wyndham Lewis' figures because they were not seen as the passive possessors of significant form, but as articulated systems in action and under stress.

There was a great deal in all this that Piper felt compelled to reject out of hand at the bidding of his intuitions, which were already informing him, firmly, that something important lay hidden in the fact that although it was Hulme who talked sense about painting, it was, none the less, Lewis who produced the pictures—but he still found in the argument proposed rather more that was helpful to him in giving a solidly reasoned foundation to the idea of a non-literary language of the eye, and stripping the Blakean concept of "immortal thoughts" of their nebulosity. It was reassuring, too, to find that in the wider cultural field to which Kenna had introduced him Blake's madness and eccentricity seemed less a matter of his weaknesses than a function of his being misunderstood. The liberation of painting from sordid drudgery took on the aspect of a reasonable enough proposition as Rimbaud stated it: "We will free painting from its old habit of copying and give it supremacy. The material world will become only a means for evoking aesthetic expressions. Objects will no longer be reproduced, but feelings will be expressed through the medium of lines, colours, and designs, taken from the external world but simplified or controlled —sheer magic."

It will seem strange to some that Piper should have found so little that was useful to him in the work of the survivors of England's pre-War Modernist movement at this stage in his development when he was getting so deeply into its ideology. But the fact is that, although many of the English Futurists and Vorticists of the brave days of 1912–14 were to recover their balance later as individual painters, they had rather noticeably failed, artistically speaking, to stand up to the stresses

36

of the War, and the groups in which they had been aligned had, quite simply, fallen apart. Piper had not been aware of their work in their brief hour of vitality before the War. He had encountered them only as they emerged from its mud and murk, in a state of aesthetic confusion. The first of the Vorticists to surface was, by an unfortunate chance, Wyndham Lewis, the most articulate member of the group, and the one most deeply involved, for that very reason, in the confusion of literature with painting.

Lewis broke the cover and anonymity of uniformed service with a show at the Goupil Gallery which opened in February 1919. This demonstrated that he was substantially in breach of his undertaking of 1915, not to revert to naturalism under wartime pressures, and showed him to have become a kind of angular realist while at the Front. Piper probably was not aware that the undertaking had been given, but he could not help but notice the defensive tone of the declaratory barrage that Lewis put up round the exhibition. In the week of its opening Lewis was telling the readers of the *Daily Express* what he had been after: "A new subject matter has been found for art . . . not war . . . but modern war . . . As a theme for pictorial art war differs from most others in that it is spasmodic and ephemeral. Today it is much more ephemeral than at any former period, but much more intense." "The artist," Lewis went on to say, would paint "the harsh dream that the soldier has dreamed . . ." This announcement paved the way for a declaration of intent based on an old misreading of the purposes of the Impressionists, arrived at by confusing Monet and his associates with the brothers Goncourt: "The French Impressionists of the last century took the life of the city for the subject of their pictures—café scenes, bars of music-halls, a family at dinner, the eternal childlike awakening of a woman, or her equally eternal, but less childlike, going to bed . . ." Etc. This misconception paved the way for the proclamation of the restoration of the subject picture: "The Artist" was to paint modern war as the French Impressionists had painted city life.

There is always doubt, when Wyndham Lewis is found in such context as the feature page of the *Daily Express*, as to whether he means what he says, or is merely talking for tactical or strategic shock effect. But he spoke in the same sense in the preface he wrote for the Goupil Gallery's catalogue, when he had no occasion to be devious. He assured the reader that "there was very little technically abstruse" in the work on show: "I have attempted here only one thing—that is a direct ready formula to give an interpretation of what I took part in in France. I set out to do a series dealing with the gunner's life from his arrival at the Depot to his life in the line. Some episodes or groupings may, for the physical interest I took in them, or in their arrangement, somewhat impair the scheme . . ." To turn from this text to the pictures it spoke of was to find oneself faced with pieces of anecdotal reportage in the thinnest possible coat of Vorticist fancy-dress. The suspicions engendered by Wyndham Lewis' immediate post-War performances, particularly by his very nastily coloured and nastily drawn Tyro pictures, were necessarily re-inforced by those of the ex-Vorticist who had become the spokesman for the English Futurists, C. R. W. Nevinson.

Possibly because Nevinson was so much less articulate, so much less a verbal man, than any of the others (Gaudier-Brzeska had always held it against him that he insisted on speaking of Vortickism and Vortickists), he had come much closer to the Cubist idiom than any English painter before the War; but during and after it he gave even more transparent signs of his lack of any real understanding of its essential principle, by using it as a style with which to veneer the surface of what were, in effect, snapshots—the visual souvenirs of his days of ambulance-driving and experiences as an official war artist—with a skin of modernity. That the leading English Cubist should have been jolted into the pro-duction of conventional subject pictures by the onset of the War was in itself an indication of the shallow roots that the Modern movement had put down in England. This was even clearer to a contemporary witness, such as Piper was, than it can be to those of later generations who have become aware of the Vorticist oeuvre through the literature, and through such events as the Tate and Hayward Gallery showings, where it was to be seen in isolation from its cultural context, and rather care-fully purged of its dross.

The impression created by Vorticism in its decay, in the years 1919–25, can only partially be recreated today by the student who makes his way to such specialised collections as that which the Imperial War Museum has to offer. In relation to the gamut of wartime painting, and the war-oriented painting of the post-War years, it is very apparent that as between such pictures as Wyndham Lewis' *A Battery Shelled*, Nevin-son's *La Patrie* (a work bought, possibly significantly, on the occasion of its first showing, by Arnold Bennett), Eric Kennington's *The Kensingtons at Laventie*, Henry Lamb's *Dressing Station on the Struma*, and Walter Bayes' *Underground*, the differences are, and were, less remarkable than the extent of the solid common ground. It fairly stood out, when they were new, that their claim on the attention lay much less in the qualities

38

they might possess as paintings than in the exterior matter of their fulfilment of the expectations aroused by their titles.

The extent to which Lewis' idea of the intensity of battle experience, "the harsh dream which the soldier has dreamed", was a nonstarter as the foundation for a new kind of picture-making becomes very evident when Kennington's *Laventie* is in question. This painting, a technical tour de force of which absolutely nothing, in the graphic sense, is made, was considered to be an essentially Modern picture at the time in both treatment and feeling. It was proposed as a masterpiece of "unsentimental realism" by those who wished to save Piper from his "unsound" enthusiasms for such as Picasso and Rouault. The picture has a rather special interest by reason of its quite inadvertent duplication of a great success of the Royal Academy's Summer Show of 1874, Lady Butler's *Calling the Roll after an Engagement: Crimea*. Both pictures show exhausted troops parading in the snow after coming out of the line: what makes this interesting is, that although the one picture is a piece of auto-biography, painted very close to the actual experience, and the other a representation of a happening painted twenty years after the event by someone who had never had the experience, or anything like it, the two present images of equal power and aesthetic value—they both go just about as far as the offer of a visual experience in one-to-one correspondence with common experience of such a scene can go.

Piper's feeling about much of the post-War work of the pre-War Modernists was very much like that evoked from him by the pictures of the Pre-Raphaelites. Those backward-looking modernists of their day seemed to him to have quite deliberately adopted shock tactics, involving the use of an arbitrary colour range, and a repertory of exaggerated grimaces and extravagant gesture, to mask an essentially commonplace vision. Their real business had, as he saw it, been with the epitome of sordid drudgery, the non-selective reproduction of a visual array corresponding to a verbal description: that is to say that anyone who draws up a mental laundry list of the received ideas about the announced subject matter of any given Pre-Raphaelite picture before seeing it will be able to tick them off one by one when they get to it. The archetype of the Pre-Raphaelite picture is, of course, Millais' *Ophelia*, a work which elaborately falsifies the painter's actual visual experience derived from looking at a model posing in a bath-tub in his studio in order to deliver as images precisely what a literal-minded reader of *Hamlet* with a Home Counties experience of nature will get if he translates the speech describing her drowning into a thing seen.

Between 1917 and 1925 Piper became convinced that the Modern movement in English painting was off the track, and that its prevailing idioms were in substance Pre-Raphaelite in character, using stylistic devices to conceal a persisting commitment to an essentially descriptive and literary vision. Hulme, he concluded, had done the English Avant-garde an irretrievable injury by substituting his word "geometricisa-tion" for Worringer's "abstraction", and had, by so doing, taken it up a provincial garden path and decisively out of the main stream by involving it in a disastrous pursuit of busy angularities without signifi-cance. To find a functioning modern movement, continuing in the classic tradition without remaining anchored in the vision and practice of the past, it was necessary to look to France, where there were painters who, while resisting the wartime pressures for a regression to naturalism, had moved on from the Cubism of the pre-War years to follow lines of development that seemed rich in promise, and which were already abundantly and stimulatingly productive of work that was manifestly important.

Piper's turn towards the French Avant-garde, and away from the more immediate, and more obvious, sources of Modernist influence close to hand, sprang almost paradoxically from his heightened sense of the value and importance of the English school of painting and its graphic tradition. This came to him when he started making serious use of the Tate and National Galleries after his unhappy confrontation with his father over the matter of his professional future. He began to compensate himself for the long hours of the too many days that he had to spend labouring at the duties of an articled clerk in the Vincent Square office by slipping away to the Tate whenever he had a legitimate reason for taking a break.

The collection he was able to get to so conveniently in his lunch hours was not the modern one, or anything like it: it was the early-transitional collection of Charles Aitken, of which J. B. Manson was assistant keeper, still suffering the consequences of MacColl's unsuccessful efforts to break the hold on its purchasing policies given to the Royal Academy by the Chantrey Bequest. Aitken's hand had been strengthened by the Curzon Committee's report of 1915, and by the Treasury Letter of 1917 giving the Tate formal recognition as The National Gallery of British and Modern Foreign Art, but although these things had brought about considerable improvement in the Gallery's acquisition policies, there was still a long way to go.

The point of view that set the tone of the collection can best be understood by reference to the book about it written by the then assistant keeper and published in 1929. Manson's book gave Charles Piper's beloved *June in the Austrian Tyrol* the honour of a full-page coloured plate, and explained in its text that all the developments in the French schools of painting after Monet and Cézanne were to be attributed to a sinister combination of exhibitionism and commercial fraud. The competition for the public eye, Manson explained, had become so intense in post-1900 Paris, that a painter could not hope to succeed there unless he had a strong element of the charlatan in him: the dealers had responded to this situation by pushing men capable of bringing off the most outrageous attention-getting stunts in preference to those of real talent.

With this as the basis of its approach the Gallery was not likely to, and did not, function effectively as a museum of modern foreign art. But if the Tate as it then was could only offer the visitor a very limited plain man's commonsense view of what contemporary painters were about in Europe and England, the gallery did, inadvertently, and thanks to the Chantrey Bequest's effect on its purchasing policies, provide as convincing a demonstration as there could very well be of the loss of direction and significance that had overtaken the English school of painting as the creative impulse of Romanticism petered out into anecdotal naturalism on the one hand, and the grand classical tradition degenerated into a sterile academism on the other. This direction, consistently away from the grand tradition, was made less obvious than it might have been by the retention of the more important English paintings in the National Gallery in Trafalgar Square, and the relegation of the greater part of Turner's magnificent oeuvre to the Tate's cellars, but it was only necessary to see the "official" Turners hung beside the Claude Lorrain landscapes in the National Gallery to recognise that, whatever might have happened later, mediocrity had not always been the characteristics of the English school.

What was initially evident to Piper, rather simply, was that his preferences were heavily concentrated at what was historically the further end of the line; but with the passage of time this simple observation took the form of the proposition that the pictures of Turner's period had a manifest importance and authority that the later ones altogether lacked: a process of trivialisation had been at work. As with all genuinely creative persons, however, Piper's critically negative reactions to work that did not please him were much less important in shaping his ideas than his positive responses to specific paintings and the works of particular painters which did.

James Ward's *Gordale Scar* was one of the specific works that rang the bell for him at a rather early stage in his development. This picture, which has since become a kind of neo-Romantic talisman, was not highly regarded in the early 1920s, and was indeed then laughed at as funnily bad, a typical example of what Roger Fry was given to describing as "the imbecilities of the English school". It was considered to be in the nature of an awful warning of the sort of trouble that local artists had tumbled into as a consequence of their taking the provincial rhetoric of English eighteenth-century criticism at its face value: they were thought to have stupefied themselves with loose thought about the sublime and the picturesque, and Ward in particular was supposed to have been fool enough to suppose that grandeur could be achieved by painting big things on large canvases. His *Gordale Scar* was written down as the ineptitude of an animal painter who had become too big for his breeches and tried to do something altogether beyond his powers.

Piper, who was originally drawn to the picture as an enormously successful topographical illustration (he still thinks of it as a superb achievement in that genre), an almost perfect statement of what it is that makes the Scar worth seeing, found that there was more to it than that, an extremely strong and beautifully organised structure of brown tonalities, with a very convincing balance of vertical and horizontal components. Piper's discovery that this mysteriously marvellous picture was not just a large drawing coloured up in order to reinforce its plausibility, and that it was "about" the colour brown fully as much as it was "about" Gordale Scar, led him on to the further discovery of the numerous *pochades* in which Ward had worked out his ideas for "finished" pictures in terms of freely brushed-in colour masses wholly unsupported by linear draughtsmanship.

These brought the sub-world of painters' paintings, in which Turner's and Constable's sketches are the leading English examples, to Piper's attention. Through them he learned to recognise structures of tone and colour in Turner's work that had previously escaped him, and he had his first inklings of Turner's reasons for wanting to have his big formal landscapes hung beside those of Claude Lorrain—not, as the Podsnaps of the nineteenth century supposed, because he wished to advance the simplistic claim to equality of achievement as a practitioner of the grand manner, but to assert that his pictures were essentially like Claude's in being "about" something other than their stated subject matter, and that they were, for precisely that reason, even though wholly English in their manner, a valid contribution to the grand tradition of European painting.

The nature of that essential something, which remained a good deal of a secret even to those who gave thought to the juxtaposition of the two men's works in the lobby leading into the English rooms of the National Gallery, seemed to Piper to become an open subject as soon as he made the connection between the finished paintings and Turner's limited palette sketches on the one hand and Claude's sepia wash drawings on the other. In many cases the sketches that provided the working foundation for a subsequently executed "finished" picture have survived, to speak unambiguously in favour of the supposition that both men initially saw their motifs as abstractions, and that these abstractions gave the picture in its final state its structure and organisation.

In his Vincent Square days of lunch-hour gallery-going and weekend Sunday-painting Piper formed the opinion that, as a result of the English school's nineteenth-century descent into naturalism and literalism, English painters had lost sight of the necessity for translating the terms of the visual array into abstractions related to the characteristics of the materials available to the artist as a necessary preliminary to picture-making. They had consequently lost both the art of speaking of reality in terms of paint on the one hand, and of giving their pictures classical structure and organisation on the other. It seemed to him that the importance of Cézanne and Monet for painters and painting, as opposed to the value of their individual works as a source of aesthetic pleasure for people looking at them, lay in their success as standard-bearers in the revolt against naturalistic, camera-eye realism: they had turned back the tide in France by reasserting the vital importance for painting of the rendition of realities in terms of paint on the flat surface, and had opened the branching road which had led, in what he felt to be the more important and promising instance, to Cubism, whose practitioners had gone on from the revival of the art of making abstractions from realities the foundations of their paintings to the momentous step of giving the abstractions themselves autonomy as pictures in their own right. He saw, or felt that he saw, that the French Avant-garde was elevating painting "to its own proper sphere of invention and visionary conception", and he came to believe that it was through a study of what the painters of the school of Paris were building on the foundations provided by the French classical tradition that the secret of the lost greatness of the English school of painting could be recovered and restored.

It has to be emphasised that it was nothing in the nature of a repudiation of the value of the English tradition that made Piper turn towards France at this time, because his attitude was taken very much against the grain of contemporary criticism. In the realm of art criticism the legitimately anti-Romantic, anti-parochial, anti-Victorian, English Classical revival had drifted into a slack-minded habit of pro-French, cosmopolitan polemic against English art and the English artistic tradition in general. The leading critics and spokesmen for the Modern movement in painting had jockeyed themselves into extreme positions in the course of an embittered row about the Chantrey Bequest which had dragged on into the 1920s from a bad start in 1904. It was destined to drag on for two more decades after that. In order to break the Royal Academy's control of the expenditure of the income derived from Sir Francis Chantrey's fund, and to make it possible for the Tate Gallery to purchase works by such as Monet, Degas, Pissarro, and Rodin, with Sir Francis' money it was necessary, apparently, for Roger Fry, D. S. MacColl, and many others who shared their way of thinking, to declare that it was impossible to carry out the intentions of the trust in the matter of "the purchase of works of fine art of the highest merit in painting and sculpture" if the proviso that the works bought should be "entirely executed within the shores of Great Britain" was insisted upon.

The foundation for the assault upon the terms of the Chantrey Bequest was a real abuse. The proviso that the purchasing for the National Collection should be done by the President and Council of the Royal Academy had made it possible for the fund to be transformed, by an easily comprehensible, if inexcusable, process, into an engine for supplying the collection with works by members of the Royal Academy. Fry, MacColl, and their allies had however gone far beyond the necessities of the case by arguing that any collection of painting largely limited to the work of English painters, and that produced by foreigners while resident in Britain, must of necessity be mediocre. There was an ironclad case for saying that the Royal Academy had failed in its duties to the trust by purchasing mediocre pictures in an unnecessarily restricted market, but those who wished to vary the trust could not stop there.

Fry in particular committed himself to the view that English painting was in some vital respect inferior to European painting, and that the English tradition in the graphic arts was a lost cause, adherence to which carried the penalty of the acceptance of a second or third-rate rôle. Something, though not much, was to be said for Richard Wilson

44

and Alexander Cozens, but such as Girtin and Cotman were "drivelling amateurs", and Turner was simply an industrious hack. The force of Fry's obsession with this issue was so great as finally to commit him to wondering, in print, "whether Turner ever did have any distinctive personal experience before nature. His vision was a means to this business of making pictures . . . for which he had an enormous repertory of pictorial recipes."

While it is easy in the light of hindsight to comprehend how such extravagances rose naturally from the intensity of the art-politics involved in busting the old Tate as a gallery for the exhibition of British art and making it a museum of modern art in general, it is correspondingly easy to forget the passion with which the anti-English arguments were advanced, and how corrosive the effect of their constant reiteration was upon aspirant English painters. It took a quite unusual degree of hard-headed common sense on Piper's part to resist the enormous pressure which was being put on the members of his generation to turn to Paris to learn how to become French mannerists, and to look, instead, at what was being done in France in the hope of regaining command of the lost element that had once been the strength of the English tradition.

This account of the evolution of Piper's earlier thoughts about painting may suggest that he was a preternaturally serious young man whose obsessive concern with the arts kept him out of the worlds of play and pleasure. But this was far from being the case. His less serious musical self was often to be seen at private dances in and around Epsom, Sutton, and Cheam, as part of the combo, consisting of Piper (piano), Milward (drums) and Anthony Curtis (tenor sax), which could be hired out for three guineas a night, and which put on dances of its own on Saturday nights in the Co-op Hall in East Street, Epsom. Rather more importantly his less serious intellectual self was often to be seen at Tanhurst House in Langley Bottom where Eden Buckle and her husband "Socrates" Woodger had valuable lessons about life to teach. These were Ruskinian and Morrisy in their general trend, and taught by example rather than by preaching, the most important of their tenets being that there should be no separation between the life of the mind and everyday life, and that one should live the life of one's ideas. "Socrates" Woodger, who got his nickname because he was Professor of Philosophy at London University, had independent means deriving from the considerable fortune his grandfather had earned as the inventor of the first kipper-smoking process that made kipper-marketing on a large scale commercially possible. There was, in fact, a brief late Victorian period in which a Woodger and a kipper were interchangeable terms. Eden Woodger, who later became Dora Russell's partner in running an experimental progressive school, was even better off.

One of the things the Woodgers did with their money was, as Piper puts it, to look after stray dogs: they kept a more or less open house for the children of their friends and acquaintances who seemed lost, lonely, and bothered by life and its problems, on the gentle principle that it was good for young people under stress to have somewhere to go which offered them the certainty of a welcome and undemanding kindness. The young person, such as Piper, who made use of the refuge that these pleasant people had to offer, found himself in what was, to an almost comic extent, the realisation of the beau ideal of Edwardian-Georgian monied Bohemia, a big bare house full of the sturdy country furniture and the unstained polished woods, beloved of the Art Workers Guild, hand-loomed homespuns, cottage china and art pottery, Medici prints and Van Gogh sunflowers, Dolmetsch musical instruments, home-baked wholemeal bread, honeycomb, health foods and sandals. The point, however, was not in what was actually there to constitute the total picture, but in the fact that when they went to buy chairs, or curtains, or boots, they did not shut off their ideas about these things but took the trouble to get objects that fitted into their notion of what their life ought to be like.

The idea is a more familiar one now than it was then, but it was a comfort in that world to find the belief in art being lived out as a programme for action. Not that "Socrates" Woodger wished to be seen to be doing anything as deliberate as the acting out of an adopted policy, he was an easy man, who liked doing what gave him pleasure and was not hurtful to other people. For him, Tanhurst House was "about" being at ease in your environment, making it what you wanted it to be, and having nothing in it that you did not want or like—nothing was there because people in their walk of life were expected to have that kind of thing, or because prestige was to be gained by having it around.

Piper found great relief from the tensions of the world of striving and keeping up appearances in which he had been brought up in the frank and candid ambience of Tanhurst, and got much solid, if unstated, support from the Woodgers at a time when he needed it very badly. The pressure on him, as the time set for his Law Society examinations inexorably approached, became very great—there was no arm-twisting of the heavy-handed Victorian type for him to contend with, just a steadily mounting, deadening, weight of expectation, freely expressed in terms of trust and confidence. There was nothing deliberately cruel or unkind about it, the intentions were of the very best, but it was none the less quite clear what the demand was for. Piper was to be untrue to himself, to murder the painter and to put on the mask of the solicitor, giving his mind and his life to a false self, and allowing his heart to pump his life's blood through his veins after office hours and at week-ends. The Woodgers saw how things were with him, and the dangers that were in his situation. For one kind of person the solution would have been a break out, but Piper was not the killer type who goes through life leaving a swathe of victims sacrificed to his necessities. The tough, Byronic course simply was not open to him.

The Woodgers could see that the only thing that would set him truly free to follow his natural bent was his father's death, and that it was important for him to come through this period of waiting for that event without coming to feel that there was anything wicked in his wanting to be a painter—since if his father were to die after he had come round to an acceptance of that belief he might be thrown off his true course for the rest of his life. The Woodgers did not even give Piper the benefit of heart-to-hearts about holding on and resisting pressures, they were just there believing in him as a young man who would some day, soon, make something of himself in his own way, radiating a warm confidence in the rightness of the view he was taking of himself, and of what he had to do in life.

One of "Socrates" Woodger's things was a knack of making people feel at ease with themselves by being easy with them, a thing that came naturally in play because play was natural to him. He had, as it happened, been attracted to Tanhurst House in the first place partly because it had been built, in a then eccentrically advanced modern style, with a flat roof, by three old men who were keen kite-flyers—they had been bitten with the bug when kite-flying, with big man-carrying box-kites, was a serious part of aeronautical research, and had gone on flying them for pleasure when that phase had passed. Woodger tried their pastime, and found getting a good-sized kite up overhead into the Surrey sky at the end of a mile-long parabola of winched line singularly calming and agreeable, and so kite-flying went on being part of the life of the house.

Flying kites with the Woodgers in an atmosphere absolutely free from reproach was a very important part of Piper's life from 1924 until 1928, particularly in 1925, the bad year between his failure of the Law

Society's Examinations and his father's death. Piper came out of that bad time with a tremendous sense of his indebtedness to these good people. It was not, of course, a debt payable to them, or one for which any payment was required, but Piper has been repaying it ever since with a great fund of patient kindness and understanding from which younger people in just such troubles and confusions as he then was have been able to draw endless comfort and support. A great many people have gone away from Fawley Bottom after spending an idle day flying kites, in which nothing much has got said, with their doubts about themselves and their own value mysteriously stilled.

At the beginning of 1926 Piper came out of the slump into which he had been thrown by his bad year, and got down to what he should have been doing all along. He left Piper, Smith and Piper, and went to sign on as a student at the Royal College of Art in South Kensington. Hubert Wellington, the Registrar, recognised his talent, but had to turn him down because he had not enough experience of drawing nudes from life to qualify. He softened the rebuff by telling him to go to the Richmond School of Art to put in a year working with Raymond Coxon before trying again.

Piper might have thought that he had been the victim of a polite brush-off when he investigated the grandly named School at Richmond. It was simply a minimally converted Victorian private house where thirty or forty people were learning arts and crafts from an underpaid and rather unscrupulously exploited staff. Coxon was working there, strictly from hunger, while he was trying to establish himself in London. He had come down from Leeds, where he had been teaching, with his ex-pupil Henry Moore, whom he had persuaded the institution to take on as a pupil-teacher. Piper immediately impressed Coxon as someone who knew what he was about, and who combined a real talent with serious intentions. "It's an enormous relief to find someone like that among your students at any time," Coxon said. "It's the odd piece of luck that makes teaching seem worthwhile—he was particularly welcome to me at Richmond, where Moore was the only other person around who had more than the merest inkling of which way was up." Coxon does not think that he had very much to teach Piper at that stage: "If I did any thing for him, it came later, after we'd become friends, and were going off into the country in his little bull-nosed Morris looking for paintable landscapes—he's been kind enough to say that I taught him how to look—and I think I may have helped him to learn how to distinguish what's there to see from what's in it to paint—

that would be about all there was to it—he was a very knowledgeable young man, and he'd done an awful lot of hard thinking about painting before he set eyes on me."

However that may be, Piper remembers the Coxon of those years as a brilliant draughtsman, who had a real flair for teaching the fundamentals of technique: he thinks that it was largely due to Coxon's help and encouragement that he was able to make it into the Royal College after a year at Richmond, and to move on to South Kensington in September 1927.

What this move did for Piper is a matter for debate in which there is a marked divergence of views. Piper thinks that he got a lot from the College, and names a number of people who were around the place at that time from whom he learned things for which he is still grateful, among them Charles Mahoney, Morris Kestelman, and Tom Monnington. Kestelman in particular has his doubts about this, partly because he feels rather strongly that the things that are important to an artist as an artist are not too teachable, and partly because he believes that the College was a very dead and boring school at that time. "It's a combination of two things: one is that Piper is a nice chap who likes to say pleasant things about other people if he possibly can, the other that we saw that he knew what he wanted to do, and had a pretty good idea of the way to do it—there wasn't much more we could do than leave him alone to get on with his drawing—he was nearly four years older than the average student when he came to the College, and he felt it— there was an awkwardness in his drawing that came from lack of practice—you could see that he had the vision, but he hadn't the manual dexterity to get his idea pinned down, he simply hadn't had the opportunity to do the volume of work that gives an artist the fluidity of attack he's got to have to get him off the level of *work*. He's grateful to the College, I think, because we didn't interfere with him while he was catching up."

Kestelman's view seems to be given partial confirmation by Piper's memories of the only two criticisms he received from Sir William Rothenstein, who was then Principal and head of the painting school. He praised one of Piper's landscapes for being "like a Conder", and deprecated another for being "a bit Nashy and Whitey", having detected what he felt to be the influences of Paul Nash and Ethelbert White on that particular piece of work. Sir William appears with more credit in another memory: when Piper told him how profoundly boring he was finding a series of lectures he was being obliged to attend, Sir

William told him he could skip them if he would give the time to making a copy of the Cézanne which had just been lent to the Tate by the Courtauld Trust: *Aix, a Rocky Landscape*.

The nub of the matter emerges, however, in Piper's observation that the design school was a great deal more interesting than the painting school in his day. He put in a considerable amount of his time at the College with Francis Spear, a stained-glass man and a lithographer, a thorough-going professional who had a leading rôle in the revival of English lithography. Spear taught Piper and his other students that the only purpose of teaching them the conventional lithographic technique was to enable them to bash it as soon as they had mastered it.

Through Spear's teaching at the Royal College Piper was able to see the very great technical interest possessed by the heavily worked-over lithographs that Rouault had been producing in his important second phase of creativity; in these fascinating productions he had used the lithograph as a foundation into which he had worked with oils, gouaches, and Indian ink. Looking at them in the light of Spear's teaching, Piper had his first clear sight of what might be done by mixing media in this way, and at the same time gained a fresh insight into the purposes that had inspired some of Blake's much criticised technical unorthodoxies. Piper's work with Spear on lithographic processes thus provided the starting point for a "family" of his own original work characterised by the use of washes of watercolour, gouache, or diluted ink over resists, generally areas prepared with waxed crayons. Piper at first made his own crayons by working powdered colours, of the kind used in making up oil-paints, into melted candle-wax, but years later found the perfect crayons, in consistency, colour range, and permanence, in those made by a Japanese firm and sold in England under the brand name Pentel.

This was, however, only a single aspect of the line of development that was opened to him in the design school of the Royal College, and which was in due course to make him one of the most technically versatile British artists of his time. He also benefited in roundabout ways from being there. It was, for instance, while he was working on his copy of the Courtauld Cézanne at the Tate that H. S. Ede, who was then working at the gallery as an assistant, came by and was impressed by his evident understanding of what the painting was about. Ede stopped to give him a word of praise, stayed to talk, and in due course became a friend. Ede introduced Piper to Braque at his home in Hampstead later in the year, and he did him what was possibly an even greater service by drawing his attention to the interest and importance of the series of Cubist pictures embodying musical references which Braque had done between 1911 and 1918. Piper responded immediately to the oils in this group, and presently decorated a chest, which is still in his possession, with very pleasant pastiches deriving from them. From the point of view of his own serious work, however, he found more stimulating the pictures in the series which were either *papiers collés*, or skilful imitations of them, in line and colour wash.

It is easy to understand the appeal of these works, in which Braque used oil-paint mixed with sand, commercial sandpapers, corrugated paper, wrapping paper, and wallpapers simulating grained wood surfaces, for a young man who was excited by the idea of booting technical conventions. His interest was so great that when he heard, not long after his meeting with Ede, that Picasso was showing a collection of *papiers collés* in Paris, at the Galerie Pierre in the rue de Seine, he decided to go over to see it. The show was well worth while from his point of view of the moment, but it had more important consequences for him than a mere refuelling of a specific interest.

Although present conditions, under which it is easy to keep in touch with the current state of any given art, and particularly of painting, make it difficult to appreciate how things were, the arts were then considered a minority interest and were not given very extensive coverage by the press and the magazines. It was hard, even for someone with as developed an interest in the arts as Piper had, to keep abreast of what the Avant-garde, and much more so its individual members, was up to at any given moment. The press and the magazines, by an entirely natural process given the conditions of the time, told the story of what was locally interesting, and of the outcome of the battles of the day before yesterday, reporting trends after they had developed rather than while they were in formation.

In Paris Piper found that the Braque and Picasso he had come to see no longer existed, both men had moved on from Cubism and were producing the marvellous series of still-lives which represent Braque's supreme achievements and one of the most richly productive episodes in Picasso's protean career. Nothing like a general view of these stunning achievements was available to Piper at the time, but he was able to gain some inkling of the huge strides forward that both men had taken from the few canvases that he was able to see here and there. His excitement was intense, and under its influence he began keeping the big Picasso notebook that has been an important resource in his thinking about painting ever since. Reproductions of any quality were then much

4   At the top of the stairs, Fawley Bottom: "Homage to Braque", painted box, 1929
Bass advertisement thrown out by The Catherine Wheel, Henley during improvements in 1936

harder to come by than they are now, and when he was making his first entries into the notebook Piper often made his own coloured copies of Picasso's paintings on the spot in the galleries where he came across them.

While making these copies Piper was particularly struck by a particular group of paintings which Picasso had painted in Dieppe in 1922, in which he could be, as it were, seen in the process of incorporating into his technical repertory the lessons he had learned from his collages. These paintings are successors to a sufficiently interesting group in which Picasso exploited the divorce of line from the boundaries of colour masses which had emerged as a characteristic of his *papiers collés*. They carry the liberation a stage further by using the liberated line to create powerful structures with a complete autonomy from literary references. Literary references are indeed made by these canvases, so that they are identifiable by such titles as *Glass, Bottle, and Packet of Tobacco*, to name the very beautiful example from the group now in the Basel Kunstmuseum, but the descriptive terms involved apply to vestigial linear metaphors which have been incorporated with great deftness and wit into harmonised structures composed of non-representational colour masses on the one hand, and areas blocked out with brushed-in *hachures* on the other.

The fascination that these pictures still possess for those interested in technique makes it possible to realise how exciting they must have seemed to Piper when he first saw them: the nervous tension of the calligraphy makes them wholly personal to Picasso. They remain his and nobody else's, utterly unlike anything that had ever been done before, and they are still unique in their force and character. What struck Piper most about them, with their curiously limited range of muted colours, and their almost puritanical formality and seriousness, was the extent to which they seemed to have been painted against the grain of their creator's natural tendencies. These appeared to him to find their full expression in the series of fluidly drawn and brilliantly coloured still-lives which Picasso began to produce in impressive numbers from the middle of 1924 onwards. It was while he was thinking about this development of Picasso's still-life family of paintings, that Piper began to conceive the idea of a disciplinary programme for himself that would involve passing through an abstract period in search of a personal style.

It is in this conception of a disciplinary programme, thoroughly characteristic of an almost puritanical element in Piper's makeup, in

53

which is to be found the clue to what many people find the most mysterious and disconcerting feature of his career, his espousal and subsequent abandonment of a purely abstract style. The translation of the idea into action lay, however, some five years ahead of him in 1927, and the immediate effect of his rediscovery of Picasso was of another kind. While making the copies for the Picasso notebook he came to a final recognition that so far as style and technique were concerned, his interest in the Fauves was exhausted, and that the work of such men as Othon Friesz and Dunoyer de Segonzac, which had begun by meaning a lot to him, and which was still proving useful to such friends and older contemporaries as John and Paul Nash, R. O. Dunlop, and Keith Baynes, was no longer offering him anything. He found Matisse wholly admirable, and has never ceased to find pleasure in his work, but the path it opened was one that he never wished to travel. The copying also closed out any utilitarian interest that he might have developed in the work of Vuillard and Bonnard: although he was responsive to the sensuous appeal of the two men's handling of colour he felt that their indifference to formal structures and absorption with surface accidents put them into a camp in which he did not belong.

He later came to appreciate the importance of Vuillard's early work, in which the drawing was done by the juxtaposition of colour masses, as a creative contribution to the development of the Modern movement, but the Vuillard he encountered in the Paris of the late 1920s was the portraitist of successful surgeons and somewhat overblown middle-aged ladies in their "luxe et cossu" environment. That Vuillard practised a species of soft focus naturalism. "If I'd seen his early stuff when I was catching on to what the Beggarstaff Brothers had been up to with their posters, I might have felt differently about him—but I didn't", Piper says. "The trouble was—do you know the photograph that Jacques Salamon published in that little book of his, *Auprès de Vuillard*—it's a wonderful thing that shows Vuillard with Roussel and Monet in that garden at Giverny looking at the pond with the nymphéas in it— they're three such very old boys—in such old-fashioned clothes—it looks like an historic document—a souvenir of the Bel Epoque—you can't believe that it was really taken in 1920—Salamon tells you how it came to be made: Vuillard and Roussel went out to Giverny to have lunch with Monet to buck him up because they felt he was being neglected by everybody, they wanted to reassure him and let him know that he was still on the map. They talked about Sisley over *canard au feu d'enfer* and Monet said what a good painter he was. Vuillard came right back to him to say, 'Yes, but he didn't have your gift for composition . . .'

"I can now see that he was a very nice, tremendously professional old boy, who should have interested me a lot more than he did— but in those days all you could see was the work of a survivor who'd lost his touch—he took one back to the days before the flood, and in the Paris of the Twenties he seemed very much finished business, for painters at any rate. You have to remember, too, that naturalism and literalism weren't the only enemies in those days—the Impressionists had really only just made it—it was ten to one that when anyone told you he or she loved modern painting the next names you would hear would be Van Gogh, or Cézanne, or Monet, or Renoir. After that you would be told how lovely it was to have paintings by people who really loved life to look at—my generation began to feel that the Impressionists had stuck us with something almost as deadly for painting as the old academic subject picture had been—there wasn't much point in breaking out of the anecdote to get involved in a perpetual celebration of the heyday of middle-class pleasures. A lot of the marching strength of the Impressionists comes from their being so jolly good at telling you how marvellous the summer hols used to be when you were young—all those outings on the river when the summers were really hot, picnics under the trees when it never rained between May and September, twenty-cover Sunday lunches on the terrace under the awnings, family life in the cool shadows under the chestnut trees, dancing by the light of Japanese lanterns at that wonderful little *bal musette* . . . and so on, and on.

"When I first went to Paris I found that Picabia was writing passionate denunciations of Matisse for betraying the modern movement by sticking to all that. It was ridiculous, of course, to accuse such a very good painter of having the mind of a retired colonial officer because you could reduce his pictures to dreams of palm trees and pretty girls in Moorish corners by a little swift verbal trickery, but it struck a chord. That Moorish screen *did* keep on coming up in the pictures, and outside the window, beyond the balustrade there *was* the blue, blue, Mediterranean; and England was going on from 'the weekend' to the Rock Pool.

"The critical tone set by Fry and Clive Bell was superficially serious— some of it actually was serious, in its own way—but there was a very strong undertone of 'why can't we have pretty pictures of pleasant things'; the aesthetics were being shaped by the liking for high living in a warm climate, and particular pictures were being given credit for being good as paintings when they were, in fact, functioning as an *aide-*

mémoire—bringing back happy memories of scrumptious summers in the sunny South. I didn't feel that there was anything menacing in the painting itself—it was pretty, and it was what those people wanted to do, there was no harm in *that*—but the criticism was another matter—it was quite deadly in its effect—it bolstered the idea of France as the great good place, the only place civilised enough—cultured enough, in the German sense—to support a school of painting.

"Fry does actually say in one of his letters that it isn't possible to paint in England, it's his argument, as I remember, that you can't establish the necessary rapport with what's visible while you're in the country— you don't see the sort of thing that will fuel serious painting if you stay at home. He never quite got round to saying that the only way an Englishman could get to be a serious painter was to go to Nice and try to find a studio next door to Matisse, but he gave the impression of thinking so. The trouble was that it did get to one—we were all looking to France—how could we do anything else with Picasso and Braque hitting the top of their form in the middle of all that was going on there?

"But there was all the difference in the world between going to Paris for painting's sake, and going there to take refuge from the quality of English middle-class life. The pressure we were under, to make ourselves mental expatriates, put my back up, and turned me against that whole line of Bloomsbury-hedonist country. I felt that slipping off into a foreign pleasure world was just too easy a way out for an English painter to take: I don't say that it was necessary for an English painter to turn his back on what Matisse and the Fauves were doing, but it seemed to be necessary for me to do so. When I say that, I mean turn my back on Matisse as an example—the paintings themselves, in particular the wonderful paintings of the War years 1914–17, and even more so the line drawings, were always a delight to me."

In the winter of 1928–9 a burning desire to get started with his life and down to the business of painting took the place of the rage to learn his craft by which Piper had been possessed when he escaped from the law office in Vincent Square. Towards Easter in 1929 he found himself faced with a choice: when he decided that he wanted to get married to Eileen Holding, a young woman to whom he had been attached from the time of their first meeting as fellow students at the Richmond School of Art, he found that the College did not approve of married students. Piper had no hesitation about what he should do, and left the College at once without waiting to take his diploma.

The pair started married life together in what, at first sight, appeared

56

to be ideal circumstances, moving into a comfortable thatched cottage with a studio in the garden at Betchworth in Surrey that Piper was lucky enough to possess. His mother had given him the property two years earlier at the urging of Eden Woodger, who had felt that it was vital for him to get out of Alresford and into a place of his own if anything was to come of his ambition to be a painter. Piper's brother Gordon, who had become somewhat more royalist than the king in the matter of putting forward prudential objections to the younger man's choice of career since their father's death, had raised financial objections to Mrs Woodger's proposal for building him a cottage, but these had been rolled back when the Woodgers formed a small building company which put it up in short order at a bargain rate.

The gift was a very handsome one, the Woodgers were percipient in seeing the need for it, and it was much appreciated. While he was at the College Piper had much happiness out of it, his friends came to stay there with him at weekends and in the vacations, a great deal of music was played on its piano, and a warmly agreeable life was to be lived there in entirely pleasant surroundings. The thing was, however, subtly wrong. It was the perfect setting for someone who could happily stick to the New English Art Club and the limited revolution that John Fothergill had proclaimed for it, and for Tonk's Slade, in the implausible context of the *Encyclopaedia Britannica*. But Piper's ideas had already pushed him a long way in another direction, and he was rather rapidly turning into another kind of person altogether, someone who, for a time at any rate, would have to live quite a different kind of life.

The very rapid abandonment of this splendid gift horse by the young couple—they had moved into a flat in St Peter's Square, Hammersmith before the end of the summer—was justified, or rationalised, later by the statement that it was Eileen Holding who did not like living in the country, but it seems fairly clear that, at that stage in his career, Piper had business with the Avant-garde that could only be carried on in the centre of things, in the city. As things in fact were, the pair managed to have the best of both worlds while the marriage lasted. Piper let the Betchworth Cottage to his old friend and music teacher James Martin and his new wife Ivy, and kept the studio in the garden for his own use as a weekend retreat.

The story, fostered by some of those who knew Piper at this time, in the light of their knowledge of the subsequent break-up of the marriage, goes that a basic incompatibility was already apparent, and that it showed itself by the fact that he was miserable in St Peter's Square, while she suffered the tortures of exile at Betchworth. The truth of the matter, however, seems to be that they were both, to start with, enjoying everything that was going, as only young people can, and that the exciting and stimulating life they were leading fostered growth. Unfortunately for the intentions with which they got married, their growth was in opposite directions, and the characteristics that drew them together in the first place because they were complementary became divisive.

A friend who knew them well as a couple says that the marriage had, in the first place, surprised him very much: "Eileen was so Bohemian, a Renoir person—impulsive, instinctive, natural and easy-going; and John was so very much the opposite of all that, gothic, cerebral, measured, and controlled—but when I'd become used to seeing them together I could see that each found something in the other that seemed to be lacking in their own personality—as they grew up, and they were both growing very fast, they became aware that these things had been buried in themselves all along, and that looking outside for them had been a mistake, or, rather, unnecessary. The marriage was a typical marriage of inexperience and immaturity, and it simply ceased to exist when the parties to it had discarded their youthful inhibitions and anxieties and found out who they were."

The history of Piper's exhibitions in these years gives an admirable skeleton to the story of his development as a painter and a person. In 1927 he had shared an exhibit at the Arlington Gallery with David Birch. Piper's part of the show consisted of derivative woodcuts and wood engravings which were well behind his thinking about painting, and as Sir William Rothenstein had put it, "Nashy and Whitey". Four years later he was shown in a group exhibition at Heal's Mansard Gallery along with Eileen Holding, Clarice Moffat, and P. F. Millard, who later became the head of the Regent Street Polytechnic. Piper's contribution consisted of monotypes, noncommital works like those sent by Millard, which gave no real indication of the nature of his interests. He was, in fact, at this time very heavily into collages and constructions, and was working on a variety of objects made by glueing string, rope, and coarse fabrics such as sacking and hessians, to canvas. Piper made some of these constructions in a rented loft over the stables of the Dolphin Inn in Betchworth, others in the front room of the basement at 22 St Peter's Square, and some more ambitious structures in a studio he shared with Millard.

While doing this experimental work, which engaged the greater part

58

of his attention for the next three years, Piper was also painting in a more conventional style, producing a considerable number of fairly close imitations of Braque's Dieppe beach and cliff pictures. These paintings, which depart from their models only in so far as they are responsive to the combined Kit Wood and Alfred Wallis influence, made extensive use of such grained papers as Braque had found in the decorator's shop at Sorgues, and of a severely limited palette, largely consisting of black, Payne's grey, grey, dark blue, blue-green, and dark brown, and, however unsatisfactory they may now seem, were undoubtedly important as exercises in which Piper worked out the foundations of his future style.

The first fruit of these imitations, which are quite definitely images of the French side of the Channel, was the discovery of the English coast and shore and its repertory of images. Through 1930 and 1931 Piper was working the Sussex shore and the Cinque Ports for motifs, and in the middle of the second year found his own voice at last while painting a picture, still in his possession, called *Rose Cottage, Rye Harbour*. The picture is not a major work, but it is a very pleasant one, and it has an incontestable signature—no one else but Piper could have painted it. When it appeared in the London Group's Exhibition in the same year it immediately made him visible to other painters, they would remember it as the first Piper they had ever seen, just as he remembers another picture in the show as the first Graham Sutherland he had ever seen. Piper sustained his visibility, and in the following year, 1933, was invited to join the Seven and Five and to exhibit with this group, which included Ben Nicholson, Henry Moore, Ivon Hitchens, Frances Hodgkins, Barbara Hepworth, and Winifred Nicholson, in its limited membership. He had been accepted as one of the élite of the English Modern movement in painting.

It seems clear enough that the rapidity of Piper's break-out owed a good deal to his having been winkled out of his easy nook at Betchworth by Eileen Holding and brought into the company of his peers in intellect and talent in the more challenging London scene. Laura Riding and Robert Graves, who were among his neighbours in St Peter's Square, became casual acquaintances, and through the Irish painter Norah McGuiness, who lived close by in Hammersmith Terrace, he met David Garnett, and entered the outer fringe of literary Bloomsbury. Before long he found himself writing a weekly piece of art criticism for the *Nation* and acting as the paper's second-string dramatic critic under Raymond Mortimer. He was taken on as a book reviewer by the paper *to p. 66*

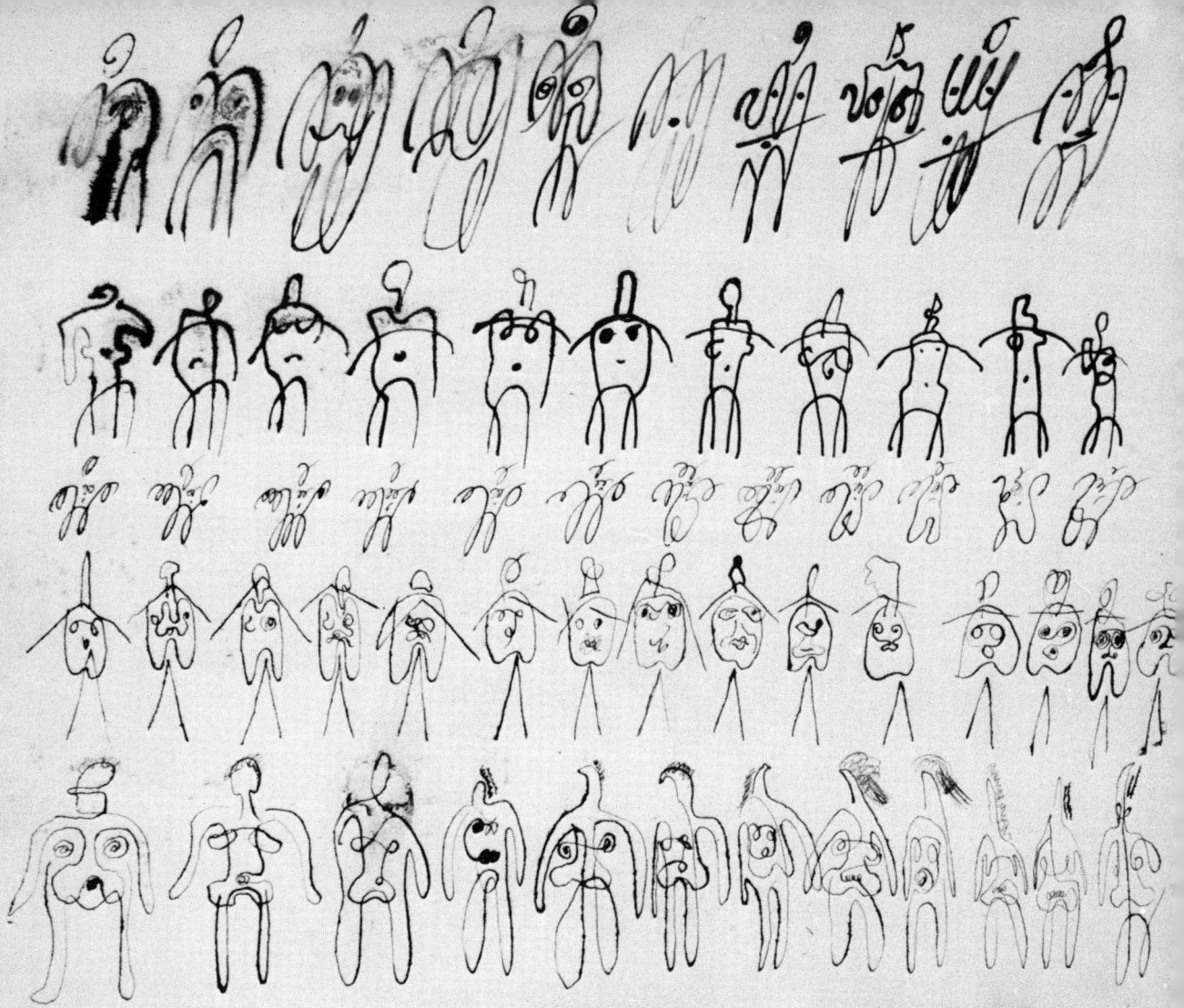

5   From a sketchbook, ink and wash, 1931

6   From a sketchbook, pencil, 1931

7   From a sketchbook, pencil, and ink, 1931

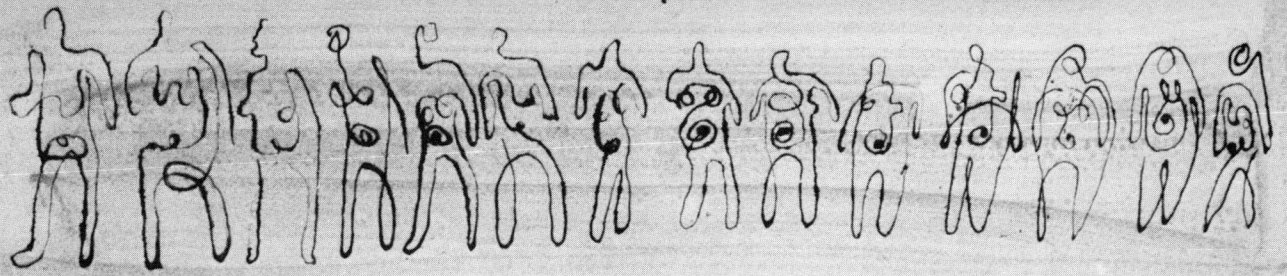

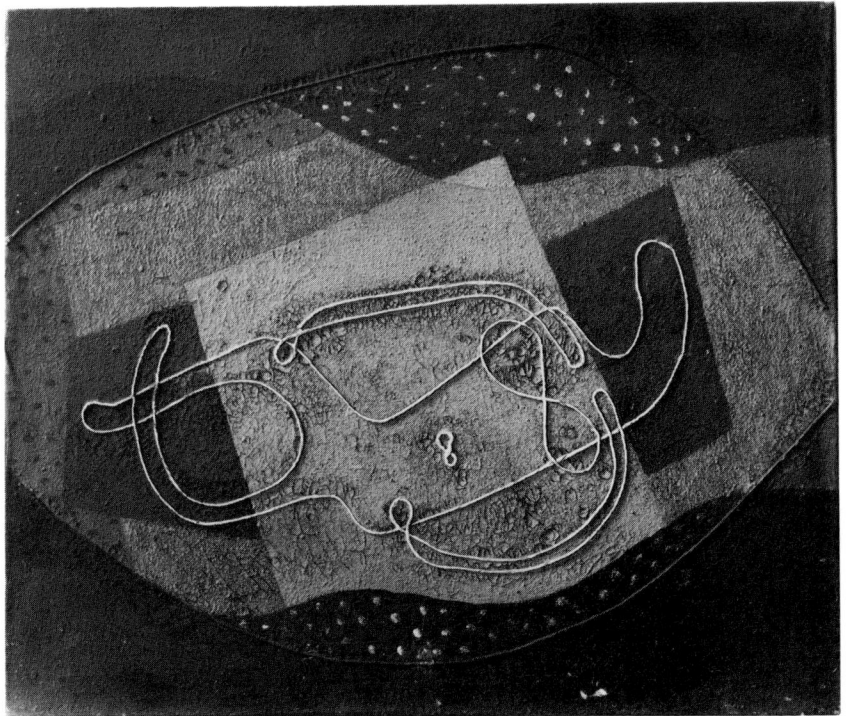

8 String Figure, oil and string on canvas, 16 × 20 in, 1932

9 Beach I, collage, $19\frac{1}{4} \times 15$ in, 1932

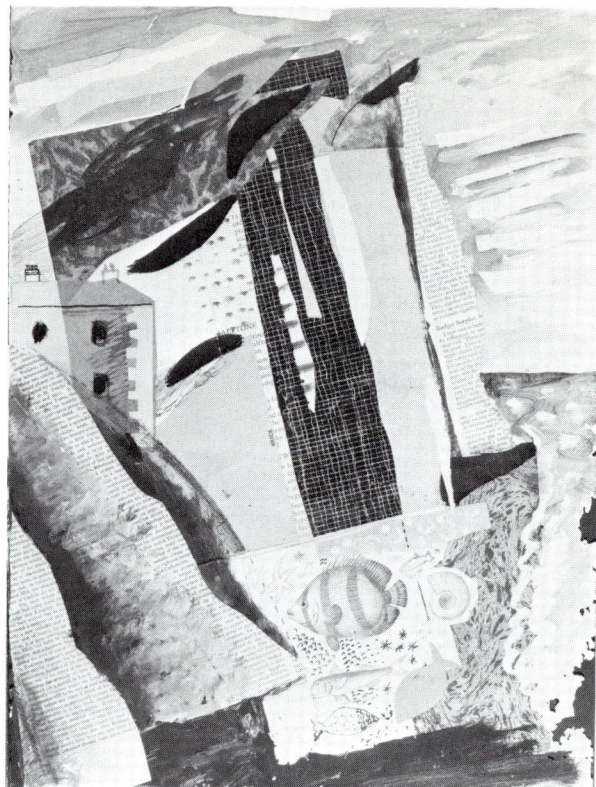

10 Beach II, collage, $19\frac{1}{4} \times 15$ in, 1932

11 The Back Room, collage with paper doilies, $18 \times 15\frac{1}{2}$ in, 1933

12 Still Life with China Tea, gouache with doilies used as stencils, $18\frac{1}{4} \times 15$ in, 1933

13 Rose Cottage, Rye Harbour, gouache, 15 × 19 in, 1931

14 Girls, Dungeness, oil on canvas, 30 × 20 in, 1933

15 Bar, collage, 1933

16

16 Construction, oil on canvas, rods and zinc mesh, $39\frac{1}{2} \times 45\frac{1}{2}$ in, 1934

17 Drawing for 16, pen and chalk, 1933

18, 19 Forms moving; two canvases in relation, oil on canvas, each 10×12 in, 1935

20 Abstract, collage, $14 \times 17\frac{1}{4}$ in, 1936

21 Black Ground, oil on canvas, 28×48 in, 1937

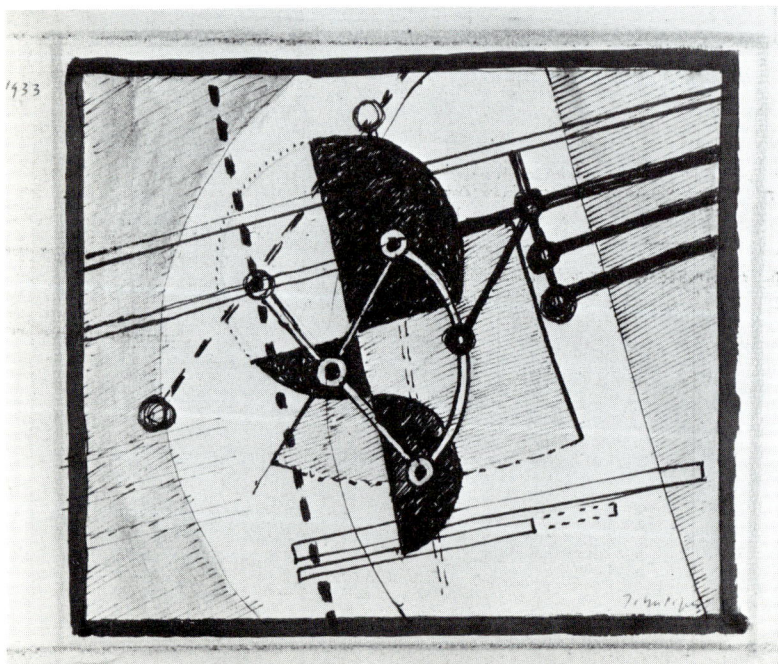

17

18

20

19

21

HOW TO SAVE

15%

ON FARES

Modern Travel
for Modern People

IMPERIAL

**Modern Art
for modern travellers**

This is what the Artist—Mr. John Piper—says
about the 'modern' or 'abstract' design
which he drew for the front cover of this leaflet

*My intention in drawing and painting is not to
imitate anything but to originate something. I
have tried to make a bright design that will
catch your eye and make you wonder what is
inside this book*

*People usually want to 'understand the meaning'
of pictures. Why? They do not ask to
understand the meaning of the enjoyment of
good food, country air, or the colour of beech
leaves in autumn—they do not even ask to
understand the irritation of wet weather at the
seaside*

MONEY

Printed in England by Chas. F. Ince & Sons, Ltd., and published in Great Britain
by Imperial Airways Ltd., London   1A/L/219 1½ m. 12/37   Sheets

22 Booklet for Imperial Airways, 1936

at about the same time, a task that in one case, a caustic notice of Cecil
Beaton's *Book of Beauty*, landed him with an enduring feud: and in
another with what seemed to him to be an unpleasingly solemn portrait
of himself by Raymond Coxon.

Piper sat for the portrait shortly after he had received an advance
copy of T. S. Eliot's *Ash Wednesday* for notice from the *Saturday Review*.
At the time of the sitting Piper had not quite got the hang of the poem,
and to help him to put his thoughts about it in order he tried reading it
aloud to Coxon, who also had some difficulty with it at first hearing.
Piper alleges that some of his friend's bewilderment showed up in the
portrait, but the photographs of it still in Coxon's possession suggest that
it wasn't as unlikable as its subject feels it to have been. The point is,
however, unhappily an academic one, as the original vanished in the
confusions of the War years.

Piper very firmly writes down the importance of the work he did for
the weeklies while he was getting started, and insists that "it never meant
more than the odd guinea to me—this was the worst part of the Depression period, and paintings—still more so constructions—just weren't

66

23 Quarley Hill, collage, $15\frac{1}{2} \times 20\frac{1}{2}$ in, 1937
Unlike the collages of 1932 in which the subject was rethought in the studio with materials to hand (newsprint, lace doilies, engravings of shells or fish, etc), those of 1937–8–9 were done on the spot, often in a tearing wind, from a portfolio of coloured and home-made marbled papers, and lithographic printing waste, especially of musical scores, found at the Curwen Press.

selling. There was no way of living by painting, and one had to keep the pot boiling as best one could. I'd hate to have anyone treat these casual pieces of mine as committed work—it was quite simply a matter of keeping going. The nearest thing to a sale I had in those days came after '33, when the architect Serge Chermayoff swapped a picture of mine for a table of his—a table he'd designed and had made for some project that hadn't come off.''

67

But the work was less important than that which it entailed, the widening of his horizons of knowledge and experience by participation in the life of a social group on which the free exchange of ideas was the accepted form of play. This may seem to be taking a little light hackwork on the margins of the literary world over-seriously, but it was not in Piper's nature to do anything without putting his best into it, and there is no doubt that the wide reading and the good talk of his literary period in St Peter's Square did him a great deal of good, both by saving him from the mental crystallisation into a world of private references and eccentric notionalism which has been the fate of so many promising English artists and writers who have holed up in isolated country corners too soon, and by forcing him to a rigorous reformulation of his ideas.

The extent to which he benefited may be judged by reference to the three articles about the English Avant-garde which Joe Ackerley, the literary editor of the *Listener*, asked him to write in the early part of 1933. These articles, two of them entitled "Younger English Painters", and the third, "Contemporary English Drawing", are interesting not only because they gave some of the artists mentioned (Ben Nicholson, Henry Moore, Ivon Hitchens, Victor Pasmore, William Coldstream, Robert Medley, Claude Rogers, Ceri Richards, James Fitton, and Frances Hodgkins) their first reproduction in the national press, but also by reason of their catholicity of taste and understanding. The three pieces show that Piper could already, with a quite unusual degree of objectivity, recognise the validity of purposes and interests other than his own, and see virtue in work that he would not have wished, in any circumstances, to produce himself.

While this breadth of view, as unusual in a young painter as in a young critic, was of tremendous immediate advantage to him, in enabling him to achieve a more profound understanding of the Modern movement in painting than any other English painter of his generation, it was ultimately to involve him in serious difficulties with the English Abstractionists who were, with the active encouragement of Herbert Read, even then moving towards the absolutism characteristic of revealed religions and tending to the belief that Abstractionism had invalidated all other approaches to painting. In 1933, however, these difficulties lay some way ahead, and for the time being Piper was on excellent terms with Ben Nicholson and the other members of the Parkhill Road group, so much so, indeed, that Nicholson persuaded him to become the secretary of the Seven and Five, a position which he continued to hold until 1938.

Through this secretaryship, and through the *Listener* articles, Piper formed a more lasting although never an easy friendship with Ivon Hitchens, a man ten years his senior. Hitchens was interested in what Piper had said, and came over to see him while he was staying in the garden studio at Betchworth in order to work on his constructions in the stable loft of the Dolphin. The visit was a success, and when he left Hitchens invited Piper to call on him in his studio in the Adelaide Road as soon as he was back in town. The return visit was also a success, and it led to an exchange of paintings. Hitchens gave Piper a picture of a ruined church at Treyford in Sussex, and Piper gave Hitchens a gouache of two nudes.

The new friendship was an important one for two main reasons, the first being that Hitchens had a short while before made the artist's essential breakthrough and achieved his mature style. He was beginning to produce works of great beauty consisting of abstractions from the visible world which made virtually no use of linear draughtsmanship or literary descriptions, and even less of metaphor or symbol. He was making his statement with freely brushed-in colour areas placed in relationships, spatial and tonic, which achieved a complete non-literary description of the subject. Piper could at once recognise that this was not only painting "elevated to its own proper sphere of invention and visionary conception" but also that Hitchens, who was a man very like him in physique and temperament, had arrived at his solutions to the stylistic problem by intuitive and reductive processes diametrically opposed to those that he had himself been following since he had been put on the Classical, as opposed to the Romantic, path by his friend Kenna. Hitchens had found his key, the liberation of colour masses from the tyranny of linear boundaries, and the release from literalism that goes with it, in Matisse and the Fauves; and he had achieved his personal idiom not by widening his cultural horizons and increasing his range of knowledge and understanding, but by an almost ruthless process of exclusion and reduction, in which everything that was not immediately useful to him in his painting was discarded.

Piper's new intimacy with Hitchens, coming as it did just after he had been reading a great deal of D. H. Lawrence's writings, forced him to recognise his need to satisfy his longings for the dark waters from Conla's Well. He could no longer deny the instinctive and non-rational side of his personality, and he realised the vital importance both of bringing its intuitive and intellectual sides into balance, and of discontinuing the attempt to make the one the master of the other. The example of

Hitchens' serene trust in the value of his intuitions had, in fact, the longterm effect of restoring his confidence in the value of his own, a matter with significance of a special kind for him since it was his intuition which had told him that he was to be a painter in the face of his father's rational persuasion that he should be something else. Many other factors were certainly involved, but the development of this friendship undoubtedly played its part in relieving him of the burden of guilt generated by that conflict and setting him free to find himself both as an artist and an individual.

Such rites of passage are never accomplished easily or painlessly, however, and at the time Piper was only conscious of floundering, and being bothered by his inability to use the powers which he had been sure of since he had done the painting of *Rose Cottage*. He is still inclined to write off 1934 as a lost year so far as work went. He sees it as one in which he fiddled around with constructions in which he had decreasing confidence, and flirted briefly with the influence of Souverbie in reaction against the increasing brutalism of Picasso's massive classical nudes. A mirror is held up to his hesitations and confusions of this bad period by the *Collage with Black Head and Flowers* of 1933, one of a large number of works of the time in which he clung to a false-naïve effect obtained by using paper doilies to stand as a metaphor for a range of subjects extending from cottage lace curtains to debased Classical ornament on the pediments of buildings. In spite of this picture's use of what is rather transparently a gimmick, it shows, as does the heavily Claude-influenced *Westwood Manor Farm*, that Piper was not as far off the beam as he felt himself to be, the masses are as well organised in the still-life as they are in the landscape, and in both cases the picture goes, as the Victorians used to say, right out into the corners—that is to say that there are no dead spaces on their surfaces in which nothing is happening. Unsatisfactory though the pictures are in the light of his later achievements, they are at least wholly under his control, a thing which promises well for his future; the feebleness is all on the surface, an underlying strength is patently there.

But while it takes a perceptive, and a sympathetic, eye to see the promise of good things to come in these superficially agitated and uncertain works, the story of the coming explosion of achievement is more clearly told by Piper's constructions. These were rather rapidly losing their fussy home-made look, and gaining rapidly in technical sophistication. More importantly, the soft shapes, characterised by the frequent occurrence of re-entrant curves, were giving way to more subtle and sensitively conceived forms in more rigorously organised relationships. The constructions were also flattening out, and becoming shallower in depth; a development only partly due to the influence of Ben Nicholson's early reliefs, but much more to their increasing approximation to pictures.

This was in some sort a reflection of Hitchens' influence. The tension in the relationship between the two men, which has at times made the friendship hard to maintain, has always been manifested on Hitchens' side by a readiness to save Piper from his worse self whenever it appeared to him to be taking charge. His exhortations at this time centred on the theme that although constructions and collages were all very well in their way, the real business of the painter was with painting. He was also stressing another point, that although the Royal College had given Piper enough opportunity to draw from nude models to make acceptable academic drawings of the human body from life, he still was not fluent enough with the full figure to make his own abstractions from it with authority and certainty. This led Piper to begin work on a series of nude studies in his sketchbook which has in effect never been completed. These nudes, belonging to two families, one calligraphic, and the other closely related to Rouault's enriched lithographic work in manner and treatment, still form, and always have formed, a major component in the content of his sketchbooks. While the series undoubtedly had its beginning in Hitchens' suggestion, it soon became something else, an externalisation of Piper's inner debate about the use of Surrealism to him, and his feelings about the ideas on which the Surrealist aesthetic was based.

1930–5 were the big years of the Surrealist impact upon English artistic life, and the grim economic situation made a great many English artists greet the arrival of this particular bandwagon with an enthusiasm that might not have been evoked by it in happier circumstances. This was not simply because it emitted jolly noises promising fun and games for all in a depressing time that threatened, with the success of German National Socialism, nastier things to come, but rather more because it appeared to provide a counter to the outbreak of philistinism and anti-art sentiment which is a customary English reaction to hard times. A great many voices were then to be heard equating the fine arts with such things as tennis parties and hunt balls, a part of the life of ostentation and display lived by the idle rich, and among the many wasteful activities that should be put aside until the problem of unemployment had been solved. Surrealism had two strings to its bow: its

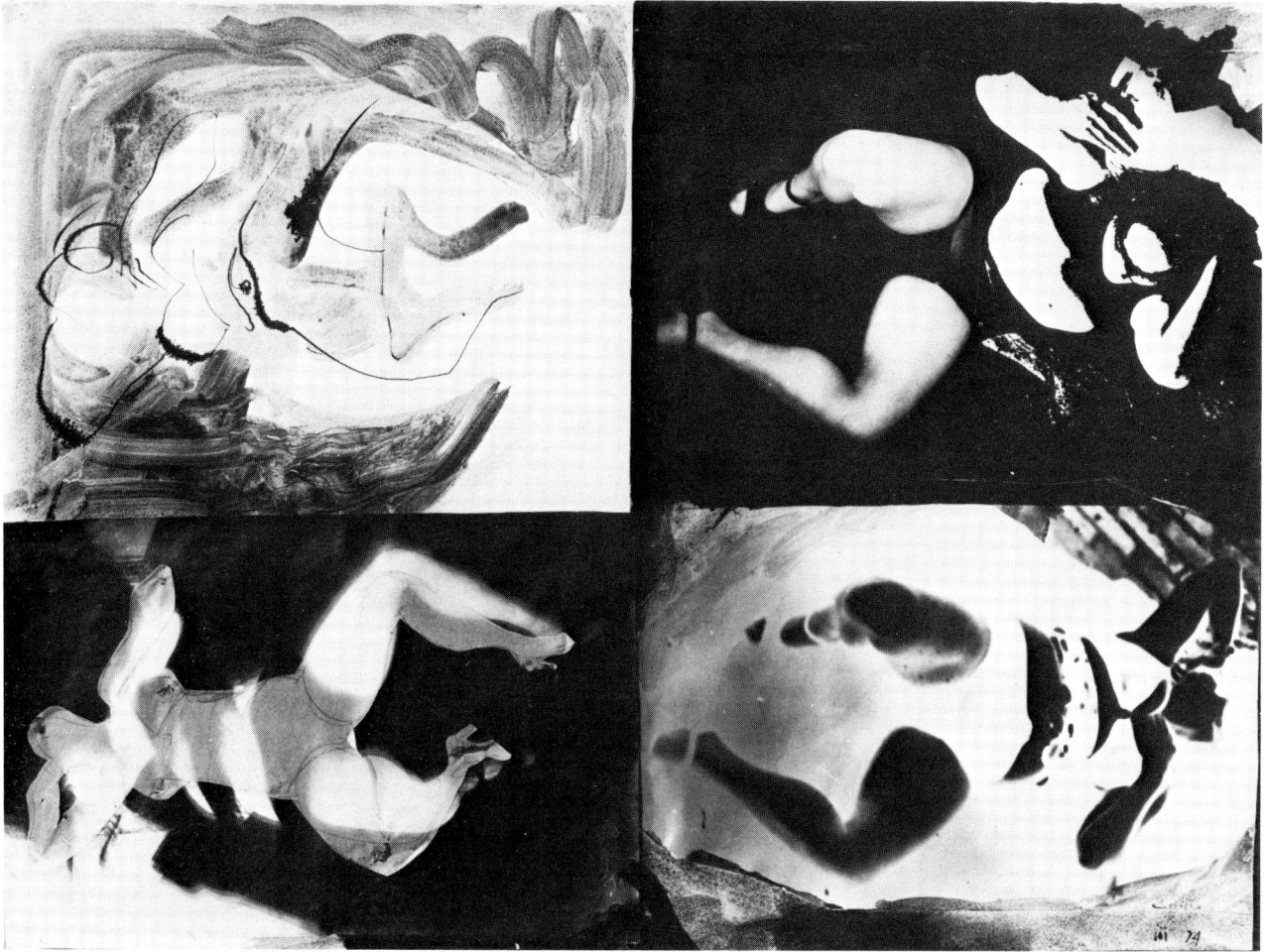

24 Eye and Camera, 1974

special rhetoric allowed its supporters to ease their guilt by claiming that their stunts were in aid of the coming revolution, while its aesthetic provided a justification for teasing the philistines and the Orwellian anti-art crowd with claims that genuine futilities, such as fur-lined tea-cups and barbed-wire pullovers were to be considered works of art.

Piper could see the superficial legitimacy of the surrealist view that it was as proper for the artist to draw his subject matter from the landscape of the unconscious mind as from the visual array presented to the outward-looking eye, but in the end he reached the conclusions that the movement was primarily a literary one, reinfecting painting with

25, 26   Sketchbooks, 1971

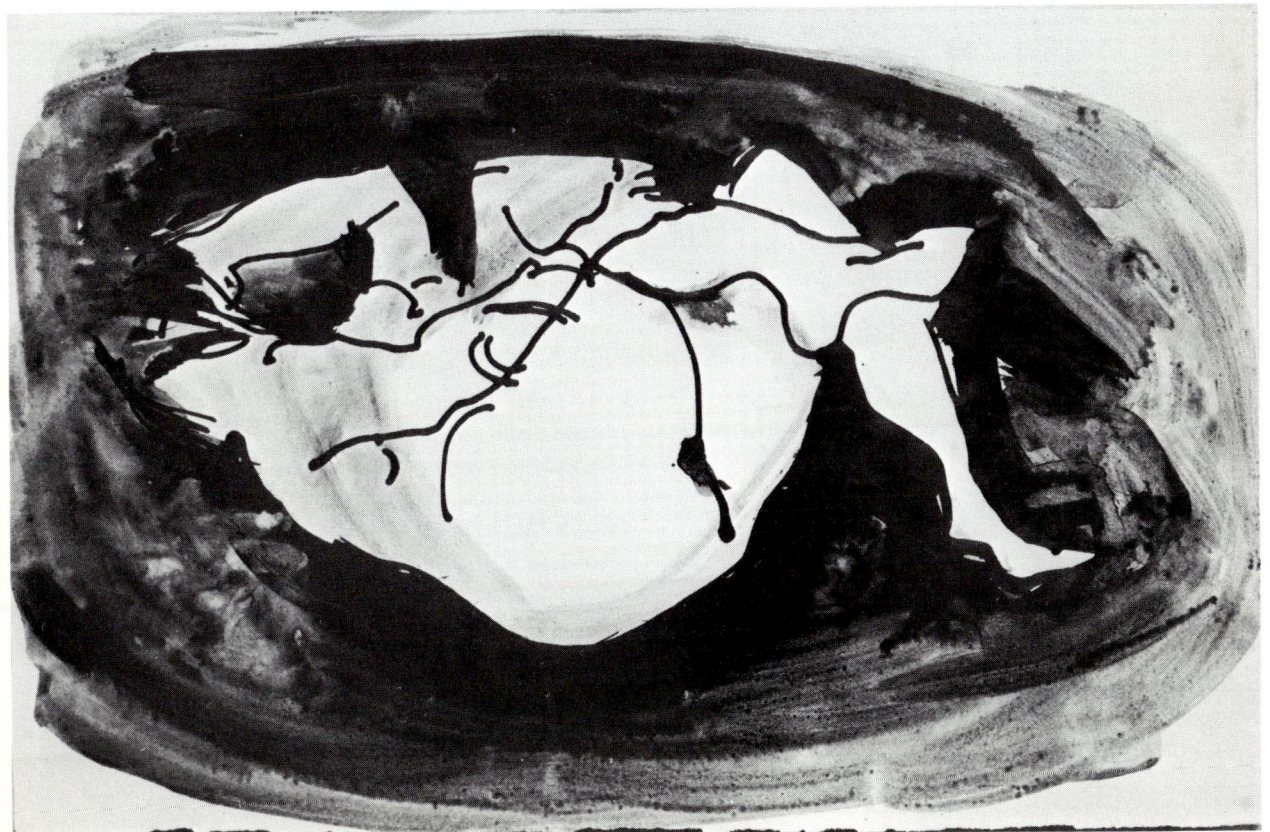

literature and a new literalism, and that its reading of the importance of Freudian psychology was incorrect. For him the significance of Freud's proposed anatomy of the unconscious was not that it disclosed a new region of subject matter, but that it extended the area of conscious control of the intellectual process. The purpose of visiting Conla's Well, as he saw it, was not to experience a high and to see visions, but to acquire wisdom.

Looking back on this period, Piper says that he made a final decision for full consciousness, and the fullest measure of conscious control. "The ancestors, for me, were Poussin, Claude, Turner, and Cézanne, their legacy was an ideal painting in which there was a proper order and an overall coherence. I'm willing to admit that this is a personal matter, not a matter of dogma. I can see that the Surrealist vein has produced great riches—that it was a productive one for Picasso, for Max Ernst, for the early Chirico, for Kurt Schwitters, for many other people—but however fine a thing it was for them, however fine a thing it may have been for others, it was no use to me. I wasn't in the mood for fun and games, and the Surrealists had their main effect on me by making me go to school again with Brancusi, and Mondrian, and Hélion." His brush with Surrealism, none the less, gave him a heightened awareness of the nature of his unconscious thought-processes, and his practice which he then adopted of probing of them by means of his studies has been a matter of considered policy which he had continued ever since.

In the end it was Hitchens, in a roundabout way, who managed to get Piper off dead centre and started up again. Hitchens saw that his friend was being troubled by something more than his concern with what to paint and how to paint it, and thought that a break and a change might do him good. He asked him to come up to his cottage at Sizewell in Suffolk to spend a long weekend with him, and when Piper had thought the invitation over for a day or two he packed up and left, leaving a note for Eileen Holding saying where he was going. While he was still at Sizewell he had a postcard from her saying that the arrangement suited her; she had been about to take off on her own too—she would be back early in the following week and would see him then.

For the rest of the summer they found themselves living increasingly separate lives. Eileen Holding was spending more and more of her time with the Woodgers at Epsom, and John was finding himself less and less inclined to leave the cottage at Betchworth to go to London. By mid-autumn their neighbours in the Square were beginning to think that they must have given up the flat, and their landlord was becoming

74

alarmed. He was in the habit of putting his requests for the rent in at the letter box to save postage, so that they were not being forwarded with the rest of the mail. Two or three months of arrears had piled up. The Depression was in its fourth year, and landlords, as a class, were in a jumpy frame of mind. Early in October Piper went up to town at last to find that the landlord had impounded all their furniture and movables, and stripped the flat. Facing the emptiness of what had been their home, Piper and his wife found it easy to confront realities. Their love had dwindled away into an indifferent amiability. Eileen Holding was passionately involved with Ceri Richards, their neighbour in the Square; and Piper was falling in love with Myfanwy Evans, a young writer just down from Oxford who was lecturing in English at Morley College, and who had come up to visit Hitchens at Sizewell while he was there. They both recognised that their marriage of inexperience had been overtaken by events: they had become different people, and the needs that had drawn them together no longer existed. The time had come to part company. The sudden fortuitous provision of an answer to this unresolved and, until then, unstated question had a releasing effect, and within a few months Piper was back on the track again. A turning point had been reached: his years of apprenticeship lay behind him, and those of maturity and achievement had begun.

27 French nonsense, collage, 1934

28 End paper for the *Shell Guide to Oxfordshire*, photo-negative of collage, 1938

II

Once a painter has found his own voice his career becomes a matter of externalisation rather than reception. He is no longer shaped by what he receives, he shapes it and converts it into his works, which from then on tell the story of his development. Piper's work from 1934 onwards might very well be left to speak for itself, and him, were it not for the fact that one of its aspects is very easily misunderstood, and has been substantially misrepresented.

It has been suggested on an earlier page that Piper had let himself in for future troubles when he agreed to Ben Nicholson's proposal that he should undertake the duties of secretary to the Seven and Five. Piper had recognised when he initially joined the group that it was in the throes of something in the nature of a purge, but he had failed to appreciate that its base was being narrowed rather than widened. He had believed that those who had been cast out had been extruded because they had been insufficiently open-minded in their approach to the Modern movement in painting, and had, in fact, been stuck with a Modernist idiom that had become badly dated: it had not occurred to him that he was being asked to subscribe to the view that the development of the movement had brought the art to a point at which it could be said that only one kind of painting was modern, and that if it was not modern painting in this narrow sense it was not permissible.

When Ben Nicholson asked Piper to undertake the secretaryship of the group, he assumed a committment to Abstraction as absolute as his own, and he felt something akin to moral outrage when he found that Piper looked on it as a useful tool, to be made use of for as long as it would serve his purposes. Piper compounded his offence in three ways: his abstractions were very good indeed, he had the intellectual equipment to argue the case for his belief that there were many mansions in his father's house, and he had at the centre of his personal life a developing partnership with a woman who had been chosen as a disciple by the French painter Jean Hélion, who was an extremely lively-minded and attractive man, and a great organiser of groups, founder of reviews, and issuer or inspirer of manifestos. When Myfanwy Evans fell under his intellectual spell in 1934 he had behind him the manifesto *Revue Art Concret* of 1930, and an episode as one of the founder editors of the review, *Abstraction-Création*, an annual devoted to the propagation of the gospel of non-figurative art.

He elected his young English friend to carry on his work in England in the spirit of a bishop selecting a promising novice for work in the missionary field. She was to go home to start a magazine of her own, modelled in tone and purpose on *Abstraction-Création*. Myfanwy Evans objected that she had not the knowledge or the money that would be needed by anyone embarking on such a venture, and told him that she could think of a better candidate for the rôle that he had allotted to her. She proposed the indefatigable Don Juan of the preface, Herbert Read, who had staked out his claim to be *the* interpreter of the Modern movement to the English with the publication of his *Art Now* in 1933. Hélion brushed the idea of Read aside, saying that she was still young and resilient enough to afford a failure that Read, as an older man with his newly and still insecurely established position as a pundit at risk, could not. With the same buoyant and stimulating enthusiasm that he brought to talking up his own, still then good and impressive, paintings, he persuaded her that she could learn, that the money would come, and that she should go ahead. And so, with Piper as her partner, she launched herself upon the production of *Axis*, A Quarterly Review of Contemporary Non-Figurative Painting and Sculpture, which achieved publication after three or four months of hard and absorbing work in January 1935.

Piper, who was very closely involved in the production of *Axis*, found the whole business of bringing out the quarterly, lining up contributors, obtaining and making blocks, designing lay-outs, organising the printing and the distribution, and raising the necessary funds, interesting and exacting. He was also, while thus engaged, much occupied with his move into the pleasant 1830s flint and brick farmhouse at Fawley Bottom near Henley-on-Thames, which has been his home ever since.

Piper found Fawley Bottom in a highly characteristic manner. He had come to the conclusion, during his St Peter's Square days, that while London was not the place for him so far as work went, it was necessary for him to keep in close touch with its artistic life. The concept of an unspoiled Epsom formed in his mind. He wanted a place just so far from the centre that it could be reached within an hour, one should be able to leave home after an early breakfast, spend the day in the city seeing people and the pictures that had to be seen, and be back home

29 Cover for *Axis* (paste-up),
$8\frac{1}{2} \times 10\frac{1}{2}$ in, 1935

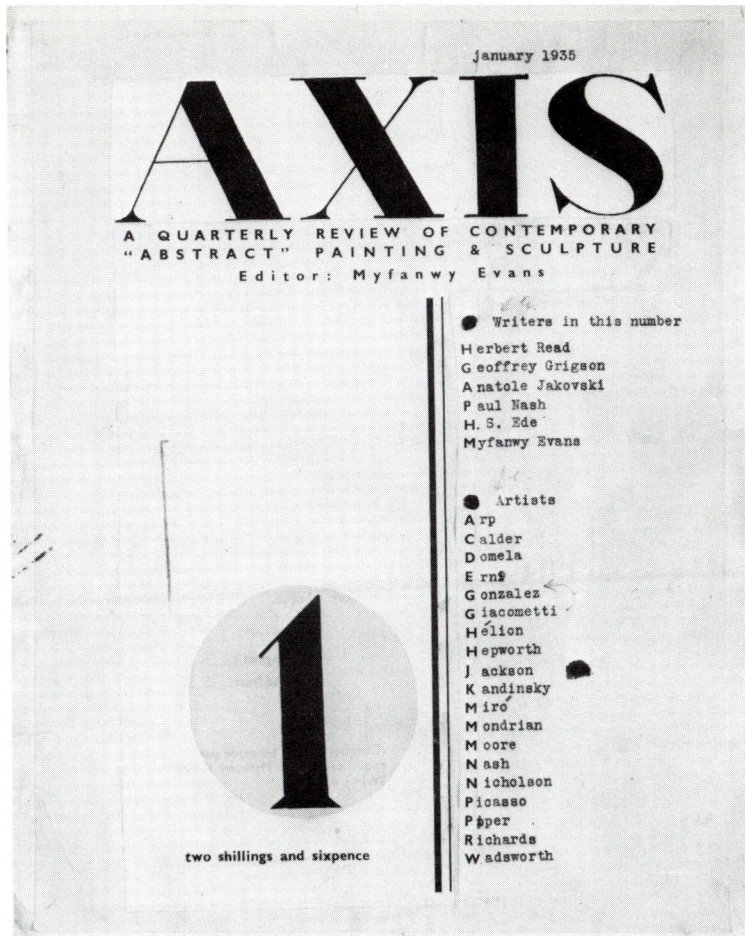

by dinner or a reasonable bedtime. Myfanwy Evans, London-born of Welsh origins, had a similar feeling about the great Wen as an essential source of stimulation for the spirit and the intellect, and a not very agreeable place in which to live.

One day, while they were discussing the problem of where, then, to set up house, Piper's sense of the practical took charge, and seizing on the one solid point that had emerged from their formulations, he picked up a compass that was to hand and inscribed a circle on the map of London and its environs which translated time into distance. The place had to be somewhere on the circumference of that circle. It was then a matter of following the line round the city, ruling out those neighbourhoods that were out of the question *a priori*, as being scenically wrong or built up, and making a short list of the possibilities. The short list proved to

be very short indeed, since both parties had so great a preference for the piece of country cut by the line lying on each side of the London-to-Oxford road just beyond Henley as to feel that it was hardly worth looking anywhere else. And there, of course, on the occasion of their first exploratory visit they found Fawley Bottom Farmhouse waiting for them, empty, in an uncorrupted and unthreatened farmland valley that has visually a lot in common with Samuel Palmer's Shoreham.

The house repays inspection by anyone who wishes to understand Piper and his work. It is not in any sense a gentry house, and could not be converted into one by anything less than a major reconstruction. Its use of the flint and brick country vernacular, and its layout and plan, identify it instantly to the knowledgeable beholder as an exercise in its period's version of the traditional English artisan style. It was built as a habitation for a working farmer, a man whose daughter might be

expected to marry the son of the local coach builder or corn merchant, and whose son would make the sort of tenant the landlord of the big estate would like to have in one of his farms, and it fairly radiates its suggestions of decent, hardworking lives decently lived. That Piper instantly recognised it as the real right place for him tells one a great deal about his self-image, if that is what one wishes to call it. Fawley Bottom could only have spoken to him as powerfully as it did if he had been prepared to listen to its reasonable and moderate voice. The house was not one for a bohemian artist in the romantic tradition to inhabit, it could only be lived in comfortably by a hardworking professional with a professional's sense of the horizons set by his degree of mastery of the processes of his craft.

Piper was to live very comfortably indeed at Fawley Bottom, but the apple of his eye, as it instantly became, was not possessed of anything in

32 With Mother: France, 1934

33 Eileen Holding

34, 35 John and Myfanwy P., 1945

the nature of a ready-made perfection when it was found. It stood empty precisely by reason of its very stark and striking lack of modern conveniences. A great deal was to be done to the house, and until the money for doing it came to hand there had to be a great deal of making do. There was, for instance, much trimming of wicks and cleaning of sooty lamp-chimneys to start with, and morning and evening Piper was to be seen bringing the household its supply of water from a well up the road in a couple of milking pails hung from a wooden shoulder-yoke. The difficulties were, all the same, trifling when they were set against the evident and complete rightness of the place, and John and Myfanwy plunged into their fight to make their dying farmhouse come alive again

82

36 J. and M. with Edward, Clarissa, Suzannah and Sebastian on the lawn, c. 1954

as enthusiastically and energetically as they set themselves to the task of getting *Axis* into print and off the ground. And although he had this full dish of bread-and-butter problems in front of him Piper was also working harder than ever, and more successfully, at his painting. With all that, and ventures into the Midlands and Yorkshire in pursuit of pre-Norman sculpture and stone carving, Piper did not have much time to consider what others might be making of his activities as they related to the politics of art and art-criticism.

What had never entered the heads of either Piper or Myfanwy Evans was that in starting *Axis* they might have been thought of as trespassers. It did not occur to Myfanwy that her delighted explorations of the studios of the Avant-garde in Paris in 1934 might be conceived of as a mere following of a trail blazed by Ben Nicholson and Barbara Hepworth in 1932 and 1933. They had then met, as she had later, the fox-trot-crazy Mondrian, Giacometti, Brancusi, and the Arps of the bone-white interiors, and they, too, had listened to the verbal enchantments of Jean Hélion as he propagated the non-figurative doctrine in its full purity. Nicholson and Hepworth had indeed been persuaded by him to become members of the international group of Abstract artists of which *Abstraction-Création* was, in effect, the house organ. When *Axis* appeared, with Hélion's endorsement, they felt almost as if an infidelity had occurred, one made more outrageous by the fact that it had been committed with partners who, simply, did not understand.

Much of the trouble came from the inclusion in the first number of *Axis* of a contribution from the pen of Paul Nash with the alarming title: *For But Not With*. Nash had appeared, as a nice young man with a strangulated talent, on the fringes of the pre-War Vorticist wing of the Modern movement, and he had matured abruptly, to become a distinguished and original artist, during the First World War. He had found a personal language, Surrealist in character, by which he was able to convert an intense literary feeling about the fear and misery-haunted desolation of the battlefields into a repertory of images. Using a restrained and dry, almost pawky, technique coupled with a cool colour range, he had organised his visions of shell-shattered woodlands and pocked hillsides so that they tranquilly told the story of the long agony that had been endured there by so many. Nash had emerged from the war experience with Celtic feelings about parallel worlds. He felt that the soldiers had visited another world of suffering, outside the world of normal experience, and as unlike it as the world of the Shi was unlike the cattle-raiding world of every day in the Irish legends.

In the peace between the Wars Nash was painting the English world of everyday as a haunted landscape, silent, ashen, almost empty of people, heavy with its knowledge of the other world of war and death whose gates were always open. In this, although his style was modern, Nash was concerned with something very remote from the aims and purposes of the advocates of non-figurative art, a personal matter. It did not seem to him that his work could be invalidated on that account, and under mounting pressure from the absolutists among the Abstractionists he produced an individualist ideology. This gave rather more evidence of the goodness of his heart than of intellectual powers, and led him to found an engagingly conceived group that had the principal purpose of functioning as an anti-group. Named Unit One, it was to be a loose association of individuals dedicated to nothing more than giving each other mutual support in the maintenance of their individual integrity. Nash's article of faith, reflected in the group's title, was that in the creative arts, "one is one, and all alone, and ever more shall be so". For him the individual solution was the life of painting.

In a moment of aberration, which he rather rapidly came to regret, Herbert Read gave his endorsement to Unit One, possibly because he misunderstood Nash's statement about the ideal member of the group. For Nash this was to be an artist who was concerned with "the expression of a truly contemporary spirit for that thing which is peculiarly of today in painting and sculpture". As a words and signs man, and not a visual artist, Read took this to be an exclusive rather than an inclusive statement, and did not like it when he discovered what Nash meant by it. Unit One, which had achieved an exhibition at the Mayor Gallery in

84

Cork Street in 1934, began to disintegrate later in that year. Its dissolution was accelerated when Ben Nicholson and Barbara Hepworth led the non-figurative purists of the Avant-garde out of it, having been alerted by Read to the dangerously unprincipled nature of the company they were keeping. In art politics, as in state politics, one purge or epuration is apt to beget another, and the purists who had scuttled Unit One next moved on to clean up the Seven and Five, by bringing increasingly heavy pressure to resign on all those members who were unwilling to eliminate all references to the visible world from their work. All painting and sculpture that was not entirely abstract was excluded from the group's 1935 exhibition, and Frances Hodgkins, who was then reaching the height of her considerable powers, was driven out of it.

It was at this point, with the purist Abstractionists riding high, that John Piper and Myfanwy Evans brought out *Axis*, which not only contained an article by Paul Nash, but also printed reproductions of work by Poussin and Samuel Palmer along with photographs of the source material of Nash's imagery. Dogmatic impurity of the gravest kind was evidently in question, and within the year a counter publication, *Circle*, was being prepared by the hard-line Abstractionists. The leading spirits behind *Circle*, which finally achieved publication in 1937, were Ben Nicholson, Leslie Martin, and Naum Gabo.

This last name is a significant one, announcing the introduction of a new element into the ideological dispute. Naum Gabo belonged to the first wave of German and Central European cultural refugees from Hitler's Germany which had come into England after 1933; he was one of the distinguished group of transients who paused there briefly at this time and which included such formidably and variously talented men as Gropius, Moholy-Nagy, Mendelson, and Breuer. This influx added immediately to the marching strength of the non-figurative absolutists, and brought out the extent to which they were involved in an international movement. There was, of course, nothing wrong with its being such a movement, but it was not long before its merit in that regard was put forward as an indication of defect in those who were inclined to depart from the pure line of the true faith. These heretics were said to be recidivists upholding an obsolete and provincial nationalism against the enlightened spirit of internationalism.

The position was not eased by the fact that Paul Nash, who was a very English character indeed, was fond of declaring that there was such a thing as "Englishness' 'that no English painter could or should try to evade. Nash's view was that a painter could neither disown his cultural

85

legacy from the past nor repudiate his visual experience of the local scene: these were the elements that had made French, Italian, Flemish, and German schools of painting historic realities, and he felt them to be sources of strength rather than weakness.

To the refugees, who had been profoundly disturbed by the Nazi emphasis on Germanic art and Germanism, all this was anathema and they proceeded to put it down with all the very considerable critical resources at their command. The English school, seen without understanding in terms of its late Victorian academic decadence, was subjected to a systematic denigration even more damaging, because more scholarly, than that to which it had been exposed in the days of Roger Fry and the Francophiles. The English graphic tradition, provincial, and eccentric, was simply not one that could support a truly modern school. The only salvation for an English artist was to purge himself of his provincialism, forsake Romanticism, and to embrace the Classical rigour and intellectual discipline of the international modern movement.

Because the aesthetic argument was confused with a political issue, and because the politics of the period were dominated by the polarities of the contending extremes of Communism and Fascism, all arguments of the time tended to be carried on in terms of the most absolute "either–or" that they could be seen to present. As the political scene darkened the cultural refugees stole away to America one by one, leaving behind them a well constructed case for the thesis that there were only two kinds of painting, that which was modern, non-figurative, and valid, and that which was not. This thesis, which had the essential charm of all simplistic arguments, that it was extremely easy to grasp, had the further strength of being propounded at a time when art criticism and the formulation of aesthetic theory had finally passed right out of the hands of the visualisers and practitioners in the arts, to end up as a preserve of non-practising verbalisers. It had, in fact, become free-floating, and utterly detached both from the internal processes of creativity, and from the techniques of creation.

A period was thus ushered in through the course of which pictures were to be looked at much less as things in themselves, produced by artists, than as attempts by subscribers to an ideology to realise its implications in visual terms. It was a time in which it was professionally dangerous for any artist to follow a noticeably individual line of development that involved breasting the flowing tide, and it was particularly dangerous for Piper, as one of the elect, to do so, since his natural evolution, divorced from any consideration of his individual aesthetic

86

necessities, could easily be represented as defection and a betrayal. As has been suggested earlier, he aggravated his offence of departing from the non-figurative fold by his intelligence and the reality of his accomplishment.

His major works in the years 1935, 1936, 1937, and 1938, included some of the finest non-figurative work that has ever been done in England, and there are clear indications that it was influential, both in its colour range and in its formal organisation, on that done by Ben Nicholson in these years. Certain canvases demonstrate that at this time Nicholson experimented with combinations of colours quite outside his usual range, and very similar to those normally used by Piper. They also show that for a while Nicholson was frequently using colour masses that suggest the vertical structural elements characteristic of Piper's construction-based non-figurative work. No question of plagiarism or imitation arises, it is simply that the influence was felt, and can be seen to have been felt. But as Piper was coming to the end of what was for him only a phase when he exerted the influence, the true believer in non-figurative Abstraction as the only path to salvation appears to have been extremely resentful at having been made to feel that influence to the extent that he did. Resentment readily transforms itself into feelings of a sourer nature, and Piper's fate was to become an unperson in the world of non-figurative Abstraction after 1938. The process was then initiated by which his name has been largely eliminated from the records of the movement, and his substantial contribution to it has been systematically denigrated ever since.

As seen from outside Piper's fall from grace was gradual. There were signs of trouble in 1937, when a large canvas, 48 × 60 in, with the title *Forms Against A Sky*, offered all who saw it the spectacle of a non-figurative abstraction silhouetted against a sky in which something was quite definitely said about the weather of what could have been either a mood or a specific moment. It would clearly have been subject to change, in a Romantic and un-Classical way, with an alteration of the barometric pressure. This almost aggressive display of unsoundness was a straw in the wind, the general direction of which was even more provocatively indicated by the essay, *Lost, A Valuable Object*, which Piper contributed to Myfanwy Evans' anthology, *The Painter's Object*, in the same year. This essay reflects a number of things, among them the development of Piper's acquaintanceship with Frances Hodgkins into a friendship that permitted a large degree of empathy.

This distinguished woman painter, who was of New Zealand origin, had had two careers. She had achieved a large measure of success as a post-Impressionist in Paris at the turn of the century, and had then broken her own stride by aligning herself with Marinetti and the Futurists. As a member of the pre-War Avant-garde she had failed to find an individual voice, and by doing a good deal of weakly imitative work put herself out of serious consideration as an artist. She survived through the War years and the 1920s with difficulty, by dint of doing brutally mechanical hack-work as a designer of commercial repeat patterns for the Lancashire Cotton Spinners' Association. At the beginning of the 1930s, as she was entering on her sixties, she recovered her command of her medium, and became a new artist of the greatest promise. She was a figurative Abstractionist who might be said to have produced her formal arrangements of linearly defined colour masses by brooding on specific visual arrays. Behind each of her pictures there was "something out there" which she had purged of what were to her irrelevances, and formalised in terms of essences, but it was not so far behind as to make the motif unrecognisable to those who had shared her visual experience of it.

Piper's friendship with Frances Hodgkins, his developing friendship with Paul Nash, and his increasing confidence in his own intuitions, combined to give him a reinforced sense of the importance of an organic relationship between the content of a picture and "something out there" constituting the visual experience of the artist. It was the lack of this organic relationship in non-figurative Abstractions that Piper was deploring in *Lost, A Valuable Object*. In the essay he owned to painting out of an imaginary locality, a synthesis of his intense visual experience of a number of seaboard environments, named as Newhaven, the Welsh and Yorkshire coasts and Brittany, and confessed to a desire to resume direct contact with his source material.

The central statement on which the argument turns is that ". . . *there is one striking similarity in the surrealist and abstract painters' attitudes to the object*: both have an absolute horror of it in its proper context. *The one thing neither of them would dream of painting is a tree standing in a field. For the tree standing in the field has practically no meaning at the moment for the painter. It is an ideal, not a reality.*" He concludes with the unambiguous remark that he feels that it will be a good thing to get away from mental concepts as the subjects of pictures, and the objects of the painter's concentrated attention, and "to get back to the tree in the field" as "a fact, as a reality". That he meant what he was saying was presently demonstrated by his 1938 show at the London Gallery, where he exhibited a number of collages. These represented real, and identifiable, houses, chapels, beaches, and lighthouses, and they were made, unlikely as it may seem, on the spot. They must be among the very few *plein airiste* collages ever produced.

With the opening of the London Gallery show Piper's fall from grace appeared to be complete. But there was more to it than that. He was maturing technically, and as his control of the processes of painting widened and his knowledge of them increased, he developed an increasing sense of their importance as determinants. His close acquaintanceship with Frances Hodgkins, and increasing familiarity with her working methods, gave substance to a suspicion which had been forming in his mind as a consequence of his close attention to the work of Picasso: in the case of the single-faceted minor artist as in that of the multifaceted major one it seemed plain to him that what came next was not something suggested by ideas about painting expressible in words, but something that arose spontaneously from an accumulation of technical knowledge and an increased confidence in the painter's own capacities. The phrase about "booting the technique" that his lithography instructor at the Royal College had used recurred to him, and suggested a model for an artist's development that seemed plausible to him as models based on the concept of the impact of ideologies did not.

He came to feel that an artist developed by quite simply mastering a given technique for a particular purpose, and then following up suggestions proposed by the technique itself. That is to say, that with the particular purpose achieved, the artist is left with the technique, about which he will think: if I have been able to do that, with it, surely I might also be able to do this, that, or the other thing. In experimenting to see if, in fact, those things can be done, he discovers new purposes. These will require either the radical extension of the technique, which is to say booting it, or further experiments with new techniques. The probability is that the one will lead to the other. It is easy to ridicule this thesis by reducing its content to the statement that an artist finds out what he is to do next by discovering what he can do, but this simplification is one that only verbalisers will find ridiculous; visualisers, and those who have worked with their hands, as executants, particularly if they have experience of painting, will not find it so.

Piper was himself prepared to face the simplification, and to live with it. He decided that for a painter to accept a verbal definition of what was a modern picture, and to form a mental resolution to paint nothing that was not covered by it, was to commit suicide: he could only remain alive artistically by leaving himself free to follow the lines of development opened up to him by the evolution of his technique. To be modern was not to paint in a particular way, but to relate what had been done in the past to what was being done by his contemporaries, and to be aware of what they were doing and how they were doing it.

The attitudes that Piper adopted in the course of his developmental crisis in the late 1930s, and which he has held to ever since, are characterised both by the widest receptivity to the solutions of their problems offered by his contemporaries, and by an unswerving loyalty to the imperatives of the necessities arising from his own technical evolution. He has done next, at each stage in his career, what his developing capacities have shown him he must do. In following this course he has abandoned the rôle of the bohemian intellectual that writers ever since Baudelaire have done their best to force upon the painter, and has adopted that of the professional craftsman whose work is at once his thought and its expression. His decision of 1938–39 was not, of course, against thinking. It was against art politics and a restrictive dogmatism, and for painting and professionalism; but it was much more fully than that a commitment to think deeply about his visual experience, and to create images that would express the meanings it held for him.

Piper's first step in the direction of professionalism was made as early as 1936, when he entered into an effective collaboration with Robert Wellington and Oliver Simon of the Curwen Press to launch Contemporary Lithographs. This was an organisation that had as its aim the rescue of English lithography from its decadence. At the end of the nineteenth century the commercial exploitation of the lithographic process had brought it into disrepute among artists, who had come to think of it as a means of making cheap, and inaccurate, colour reproductions of works produced by other methods. The situation had arisen in which an artist faced with a specific commission to produce a lithograph would execute an original design in another medium which he would hand over to a professional commercial lithographer much as a writer would hand his manuscript over to a printer. In spite of the efforts to counter this development made by the graphics departments of a number of art schools, and in spite of the lively state of the art in Germany and France, English artists were still exceedingly shy of the process in the 1930s. The attempt to bring lithography back which had been launched by the Pennells and others just before the First World War had petered out, leaving very little trace of its passing outside the back numbers of *The Studio*.

By commissioning a number of artists to create original works directly on lithographic stones for their organisation, Piper and Wellington hoped to revive the revival of the auto-lithograph. The actual work, which involved a good deal of on-the-job training for the artists taking part in the venture, was done in the printing works of the Baynard and Curwen Presses, and Piper was very much impressed by the fluency with the medium possessed by the printers. They could achieve, virtually effortlessly, effects that only came to the artists after much time-consuming fumbling. The observation is in itself in the nature of a truism, but the point was not that knowing all there was to know about the process made the work much easier to do, but that the professional level of skill gave the man who had it a much wider range of options, and a much deeper understanding of the possibilities inherent in the medium.

Piper now looked at Rouault's "enriched" lithographs with a renewed interest, realising not only how they had been done, but also the nature of the possibilities on which they opened a door. He found, too, that the experience of working with the printers had made him aware of other instances of creative correlations between a knowledge of professional techniques and the results subsequently obtained by artists who had, for one reason and another, been compelled to take their possibilities and their limitations into account. It struck Piper with special force that the technical knowledge of textile printing processes that Frances Hodgkins had acquired in her years of hardship after the First World War, when she was designing blocks for the Cotton Spinners' Association, had been extremely useful to her in helping her to find the style which had released her into her final phase of creativity; the knowledge was there, in her later paintings and gouaches.

Piper's realisation of the extent to which Frances Hodgkins had profited from her servitude brought him a further insight into the nature of the generally underrated Raoul Dufy's achievement. Piper, who had always found Dufy's work witty, agreeable and interesting, was tremendously impressed by the enormous mural done by Dufy for the Palace of Electricity in the Paris Exhibition of 1936. This took the form of a huge group portrait of all the experimenters, inventors, theorists, engineers, and entrepreneurs who had ever made significant contributions to applied and theoretical electronics, and was so arranged as to be a narrative history of the field. The light and cheerful manner in which this formidable subject had been treated prevented many of those who were crowding to see Picasso's *Guernica* in the Spanish Pavilion on the other side of the river from recognising it as the artistically serious performance that it was. Piper was struck both by the astonishingly able way in which Dufy had retrieved a seemingly hopeless artistic situation by organising his army of figures into a unified composition that pulled the vast wall area together as a single picture, and by the brilliant use he had made of lessons learned from multi-block textile printing in solving his problem; but what impressed Piper most of all was the extent to which the painter had accommodated himself to his brief while yielding nothing to it. He had produced something gay and entertaining that was appropriate to the fair ground atmosphere of the exhibition, but without condescension. Frivolous as it was at first sight, it was, as painting, at the level of his very best work.

The lesson of Dufy's picture, that professionalism need involve no sacrifice of integrity, and could bring the artist opportunities for performance and experiment that were unlikely to come from ploughing a loner's path against the social grain in the traditional bohemian manner, was not lost on Piper. He recognised that what Dufy had done, to see an apparently limiting and confining commission as an occasion to rise to, and to make his own, was what painters normally have done throughout the history of Western painting, and that his attitude was the one that had led to the creation of the majority of its enduring masterpieces. The recognition that this was so was part of a general shift in Piper's thinking that was to lead to his becoming a member of the Church of England in the course of 1939—he was coming to have increasing doubt about the Byronic conception of the arts as an expression of the primacy of the individual will, and a deepening conviction that a realistic appreciation of the bounds and limitations placed upon it by the human condition was more likely to lead to the realisation of the artist's potential. In the years between 1936 and 1939 he ceased to aspire to be an artist in the bohemian sense of the word, and became a craftsman, resolved, without any hint of priggishness, to live out his days, humble before God and his craft, fulfilling his Christian duty to make full use of the talents with which he had been endowed in whatever circumstances he might be given the opportunity to use them.

The background to this evolutionary change in Piper's conception of his rôle was a happy one. While it was taking place Fawley Bottom ceased to be a nice old farmhouse with possibilities and became the Pipers' home. Piper had married Myfanwy Evans in 1937, and the first of their four children, a boy, was born in 1938, the year in which he was given his first one-man show by the London Gallery. His sense that the floating years were over, and that he had solid ground under his feet at last, was reinforced when the work that he had been doing for the *Architectural Review* since 1936 bore unexpectedly important fruit.

The series of articles commissioned for that magazine by Jim Richards, on such subjects as "England's Early Sculptors", "The Nautical Style", "The Bath Road", "Towers in the Fens", and "Colour in Building", had attracted the attention of another of its contributors, John Betjeman, who, having become the general editor of the Shell County Guides, asked Piper to undertake the Oxfordshire volume. While this project was in the course of execution, what had been an agreeable acquaintanceship became a close friendship which later on, when the Shell Guides had migrated from the house of Batsford to Faber and Faber (after an unsponsored interlude as Murray's Architectural Guides), formed the base for an outstandingly successful joint editorship.

This development was of considerable importance to Piper in the short term and the long, as it stimulated the revival of his topographical interests and financed an exploration and penetration of the English scene of an intensity and range that few artists have been able to undertake. In "working" Oxfordshire for the Shell Guide of 1938 Piper took hundreds of photographs and filled half a dozen sketchbooks with annotated landscape and architectural drawings. Some of these drawings were cursory, the merest linear indications of the nature of the thing seen, but more and more often as the work progressed they came out as profoundly considered and brilliantly executed analytical studies of substances and essences. The sketchbooks, along with the impressive photographs that Piper was beginning to take at this time, show how he was revelling in this licensed resort to the sustenance that he had been deliberately denying himself in his abstract period, and make it clear that it was vital to him to be able to feed his imagination through his eye, and to incorporate his visual experience in his painting.

The fieldwork for the Oxford Guide was followed by just as intensive and thorough exploration of Shropshire, this time in the company of the general editor who had decided that the county called for a collaboration. Piper gained a great deal from this intimate working association with a poet who, whatever his carefully maintained public persona and his lighter verse may suggest to the contrary, combines a profound seriousness with a refined sensibility. Betjeman's visual images show how much the thing seen has always meant to him, and Piper's further acquaintance, in the field, with what may be called Betjeman's negotiating platform—originally based, as was his own, on an adolescent use of an interest in antiquarian ecclesiology as a means of escape from *to p. 104*

English Romanesque (photos J.P.), 1930s   **37**   Wormington, Gloucestershire: crucifixion
38   Ampney St Peter, Gloucestershire: erotic figure   **39**   Barton le Street, Yorkshire: panels
over the north door   **40**   Kirkburn, Yorkshire: font

41

42

English and Welsh nonconformist chapels
(photos J.P.)

41 Rhydygwin, Cardiganshire

42 Aberystwyth, Cardiganshire

43 Cote, Oxfordshire (1937)

43

a

b

c

44 Nonconformist chapels drawn for line reproduction in "First and Last Loves" by John Betjeman, 1952 **a** Kilgetty, Pembrokeshire **b** Between Cardigan and Aberaeron **c** Lady Huntingdon Chapel, Worcestershire **d** Legbourne, Lincolnshire

45 Llangloffan, lithograph, $23\frac{1}{2} \times 22\frac{1}{2}$ in, 1964

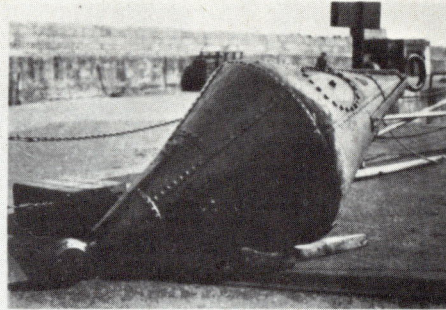

The utilitarian objects associated with nautical activities show nautical design at its simplest and most characteristic. The uncompromising geometry and restricted symbolic colouring of the standard Trinity House buoys are here seen echoed in the more romantic structure of a signal mast that stands on the harbour jetty at Penzance to give warning of navigation conditions. The form of the nautical object is severe and the architectural quality is evocative rather than decorative.

On the ends of piers and on beaches a
wide variety of objects and structures
show this same spare geometrical quality.
Four typical specimens : a harbour light
at Ramsgate, an iron harbour mark at
Port Isaac, a wooden pole for observation
at Penzance, and a speed-testing mark on
the Chesil Beach.

The nautical object has the quality
of being able to assimilate foreign
architectural idioms without losing
its own characteristic style. Here
are two pierhead lighthouses : one,
at St. Ives in Cornwall, of typical
maritime architectural form, and
another, at Weymouth, that has
based its design on the more sophisticated architecture of the Victorian
seaside but still preserves its
nautical spareness and gaiety.

47 Rycote (photo J.P.), 1937

48 Scarecrows (photos J.P.), 1938–77

49 Maze at Somerton, Oxfordshire (photo J.P.), 1937
50 Rubbing: Botallack mine, Cornwall, 1935

51 Slate gravestone rubbings, Cornwall
52 Painted farm-cart, Oxfordshire; survival not revival (photo J.P.), 1937

a home environment in which he couldn't feel altogether comfortable intellectually—gave him an access of confidence in his own approach. The poet's eye fed on what was valued by the painter's, both when recollected and present visual experience was in question, and the great good places of their creative imaginations were very much in harmony. The importance of the thing seen in the poet's work strengthened Piper's developing sense of the legitimacy, and the propriety, of maintaining a relationship between the visible stuff "out there" that held so much meaning for him and the created images in his work.

Both men benefited from the collaboration; it was not only refreshing to their daily selves as very good fun, it also contributed to their aesthetic maturation. It had a great deal to do with the deepening seriousness of Betjeman's poetic as opposed to public performances, and to the stabilisation of their hierarchies of values. While working together the two men learned more than they were aware at the time about what was of fundamental importance to them. In Piper's case the collaboration had a powerful indirect technical influence: both men were interested in the literary precedents for the kind of work in which they were involved, and both, having first become collectors of early nineteenth-century guidebooks and travellers' vademecums, went on to investigate the literature of the picturesque which had burgeoned from the developing consciousness of the beauties of natural landscape in aesthetic circles in the seventeenth and eighteenth centuries.

Piper found the technical processes that had been used by the illustrators of this literature just as stimulating as he had found the technical side of the work of the Beggarstaff Brothers at an earlier stage in his development. He was initially especially impressed by the late eighteenth- and early nineteenth-century aquatint illustrations: while these were often more than superficially attractive by virtue of their content, and the "period" quality of their vision, they were invariably fascinating to Piper because of their essential character—an aquatint must involve an interpretation of its content in terms of the specific process by which it is produced. As this is basically a matter of the production of tone masses of deepening intensity by successive immersions of a copper plate in acid, it requires the artist making it to see his subject as a figurative abstraction before he sets to work. While looking at the illustrations to the publications of such theorists of the picturesque as Gilpin, Price, and Knight, Piper unexpectedly came on useful clues to a plausible personal solution to the technical problem of using his non-figurative experience in handling images of the visible world.

This unanticipated consequence of the guidebook commitment first produced the Brighton Aquatints of 1938–9, in which Piper made extremely happy use of the process itself, and then the group of beautiful watercolours done at Thomas Jones' Hafod in 1939. These most successful landscapes fascinatingly develop in another medium the lessons learned while Piper was working on the aquatints, and prepare the way for the group of highly stylised oils done in 1939–40 at such classic sites as Byland Abbey, Fonthill, Stourhead, and Milton Abbas, which included some of his most powerful and expressive work.

The origins of the English cult for the picturesque as it manifested itself in the days of Gilpin and Uvedale Price can be traced back to a specific source in the memorandum of 1709 in which Vanbrugh gave his reasons for advocating the preservation of Woodstock Manor. In its key passage he says, among other things, that, if planted about with fine yews and hollies, the old manor when seen from the new "would make one of the most agreeable objects that the best of landskip painters can invent". The created landskip that had captured Vanbrugh's imagination, and which he conceived of realising, with parkland as his medium, was, of course, that consisting in its essence of the Campagna as presented to the European mind by the technique brought to its peak approximately seventy-five years earlier in the work of Poussin and Claude. The created landscape itself was manifested as such to the public at large in the oil-paintings of the two painters, and it was presented rather differently, as the product of a technique, in their superb brush drawings in sepia bistre or Indian ink washes with pen and ink or chalk accents.

Piper was brought back to these marvels, which he had always admired, by way of the literature of the picturesque on the one hand, and by the challenges of stage design on the other. The work he did for the Group Theatre's production of Stephen Spender's *Trial of a Judge* in 1938 had excited and pleased him, but had left him with a feeling that he had made a leap into the dark. Characteristically he felt the need to acquaint himself with the tradition of the art, and studying the undoubted successes of his predecessors in the field brought himself rather rapidly face to face, as must happen with anyone English who is thinking about problems of stage design, with Inigo Jones' work. This means, ultimately, that he found himself thinking about the seventeenth-century accented wash drawing as a means to the particular end of translating a staging problem into a visible image as an incident in formulating its solution. The realisation that Jones had been thinking

105

with his technique while he was doing his working drawings threw new light on the beloved Poussin and Claude drawings, in which technique and thought had so triumphantly become one: Piper saw in them the visible representation of their thought about what meant most to them in the world of their experience and delight. His recognition of their achievement was decisive in the formulation of his final ambition, to perfect as personal a mode to express what spoke most pressingly to him, through his eyes.

Piper was pushed in the direction of this conclusion by a suspicion that entered his head about the probable meaning of the observation from Degas reported by Walter Sickert, that a painter who means to accomplish his aims must learn to walk round gauntlets. Piper took it to mean that the only challenges that the artist can properly be called upon to take up are those generated from within in the course of his own artistic development. It is a waste of spirit for him to meet externally generated challenges, and to attempt to produce work conforming to ideological and social requirements formulated by others in response to their own pressing necessities and irrelevant to his own. The requirement that was pressed on Piper, from the general direction of the Parkhill Road and St Ives most notably, was that he should be modern, and be that in a particular way. It did not appear to him that the acceptance of a frame of reference and vision so alien to his own in its exclusiveness could constitute a valid approach to his problems.

It occurred to him, as he debated the question of modernity inwardly, that the bistre drawings by Claude and Poussin that he found increasingly admirable, and which had been in their temporal context the essence of the modern, had been forward-looking only in the manner of their execution. They had taken the exhausted technical conventions of contemporary drawing, the note-taking idiom of every hack landscape painter of the time, and had revitalised them by making the idiom the vehicle for the expression of their own, intensely personal, experience of Rome, of the Roman landscape, and the Roman light. Piper was very much struck by the remark of Claude's sketching companion Standrart that "whereas I was only looking for good rocks, trunks, trees, cascades, buildings, and ruins, which were useful to me as fillers for history paintings, he on the other hand painted the view from the middle to the greatest distance, fading away towards the horizon and the sky for its own sake". It had been, in fact, his visual experience of the thing itself that old Orrizonte, as Claude's Roman friends liked to call him, had been recording on his forays into the Campagna, and it was this direct organic relationship with the stimulus to his creative imagination that enabled him to achieve his innovative leap forward.

While Piper was learning the lesson of the Claude drawings he was also rediscovering Turner for his own use. This time he was not faced with the inspired genius looking inwards to see visions of colour that were incomprehensible to the painters and public of his generation, but with the restless and tireless experimenter with techniques, the Turner who developed a brilliantly innovative and entirely personal mode of expression by giving his concentrated attention to the conventions of oil-painting techniques as he knew them to have been observed by Richard Wilson and Reynolds, and as he believed them to have been honoured by Claude. The Turner Piper now admired had not only booted the technique of watercolour-painting by applying to it the lessons he had learned from the past of oil-painting, he had gone on from there to explode the technique of oil-painting by applying to it the knowledge that he had derived from his revolutionary use of watercolour. It was not by thinking about ideas about painting, but by examining the possibilities inherent in painting as a craft that Turner had become the most modern of the painters of his day—Payne Knight's man of the future who was to consider nature as nothing but light variously modified. It presented itself very forcibly to Piper that Turner had reached his level of distinction not by going for verbally defined goals, but by searching for the means to achieve certain atmospheric effects that he had experienced and had recognised in Claude's pictures. Groping towards the essence of his experience by painting into wet washes, by rubbing through his surfaces to the white paper below in one medium, and by rubbing transparent glazes off thickly painted white grounds in another, he had broken through into a new realm of vision and expression.

Piper's view of Turner was made explicit shortly after the outbreak of the war of 1939–45 when he was commissioned, by an editor who—although sympathetic enough—did not quite understand his positions, to write the text for the volume *British Romantic Artists* in the propaganda series *The British People in Pictures*. However it may have originally been conceived, the series provided a wide variety of writers, artists, and poets, with an opportunity beyond which it was easy to rise, and in producing a distinguished piece of introductory criticism Piper rose further above it than most. It is interesting that for the purposes of this essay he is careful to place Turner, and Girtin who was so greatly admired by him, outside the Romantic movement, and that he stresses

Brighton Aquatints, 1938–39 (Duckworth, 1939)

53 Brighton from the station yard with St Peter's

54 St Bartholomew's

55 Regency Square from the West Pier

the point that their aims were both more painterly and more significant than those of any painters whose work or ideology placed them within it. He quotes, with evident approval, Ann Dart's account of the young Turner precisely because it divorces him from the verbalisations and the bohemianism that characterised the Romantic approach. Turner was, as it were, switched off when not painting—his existence was painting, and thinking what he would paint next when he was not actually at work. ". . . He would talk of nothing but his drawings, and of the places to which he would go for sketching. He seemed an uneducated youth, desirous of nothing but improvement in his art. He was very difficult to understand, he would talk so little . . . He was sedate and steady, he did not in the evenings go out except with our family. and mostly we staid at home, and Turner would sit quietly apparently thinking, not occupied in drawing or reading. He was not at all polite . . ." To Ann Dart's account of this antithesis of the nineteenth-century studio painter Piper adds the comment "Turner's plan, as it developed, was to become more proficient than anyone else alive at any

manner of painting he thought important". He goes on from this to give one of the few accounts of Turner's career that makes sense, because it is written in terms of his technical development as it is visible to a painter.

Piper's mature recognition of what Turner had been about, a matter that occupied a large and thrilling part of his intellectual life between 1937 and 1941, formed a turning point in his own career, bringing about a species of release into fluency. His last impediments of guilt and doubt on the propriety of his chosen path seemed to fall away, and he settled down to get on with the job of his choice in the manner of a runner getting into his stride.

The first outward and visible signs of this release in Piper's oils came in the series of misleadingly romantic paintings of ruinous and dilapidated cottages painted in 1941–2. The subject matter with which they deal has led many to see in them a regressive visit to the Palmer country, but they are, while in fact in Wiltshire and the chalk country of southern England, mentally in Piper's vision of Claude's Arcadia. However that to p. 119

56 The Gorge, Hafod, watercolour, $14\frac{3}{4} \times 19\frac{3}{4}$ in, 1939

57 Hafod, "He made the wilderness smile", monotype, $14\frac{3}{4} \times 19\frac{3}{4}$ in, 1939

58, 59 Two views of Llyn Teifi, monotypes, $14\frac{3}{4} \times 19\frac{3}{4}$ in, 1939

These monotypes are part of an exploration of 19th-century topographical books and the picturesque tradition

58

59

60 English Lake, oil on canvas, $9\frac{1}{2} \times 14\frac{1}{2}$ in, 1939

Official Art: **61** Windsor Castle:
first sketch for one of a series
commissioned by H.M. The
Queen, now The Queen Mother,
ink and watercolour, $16\frac{1}{2} \times 35$ in,
1942

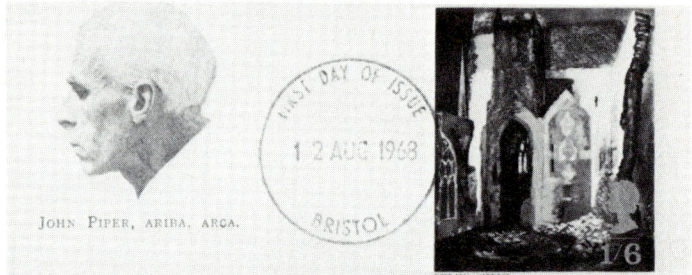

JOHN PIPER, ARIBA, ARCA.

LAST DAY OF ISSUE
1 2 AUG 1968
BRISTOL

1/6

PIPER 1940 HARRISON

62

63

John Piper

65

Recording Britain: Pilgrim Trust, wartime scheme   64   Chancel arch, Stanton Low,
Buckinghamshire   65   Tithe Barn, Great Coxwell, Berkshire, both ink and watercolour, 16 × 20 in, 1940

War Art: 62   St Mary le Port, Bristol (oil on canvas, 1940) reproduced on a postage stamp,
detail of first day cover, 1968   63   Lansdowne Proprietory Chapel, Bath, after bombing, ink,
watercolour and chalk, May 1942   66   All Saints, Knowle, Bristol, the day after bombing, ink
and gouache from sketchbook, 1940   67   American locomotives awaiting shipment on the
foreshore, Cardiff   68   Corvette under construction, Bristol, both ink, watercolour and chalk, 1944

67

68

69 Byland Abbey I, oil on canvas, 20 × 24 in, 1940

70 Byland Abbey II, oil on canvas, 18 × 22 in, 1940 (cf figs 18, 19)

71   Bolsover Castle, oil on canvas, 20 × 24 in, 1944

72   The Lower Lake, Renishaw, ink and watercolour, 1944

73

74

73 Ruined cottage, Hampshire, oil on board, 28 × 36 in, 1942

74 Derelict cottage, Llanthony, oil on board, 1941

75 Ruined cottage, sketchbook, 1941

76 Ruined barn, sketchbook, 1941

75

76

77 Vale of Clwyd, watercolour, 15 × 20 in, 1940

78 Grongar Hill, oil on board, 12 × 16 in, 1942

may be, these pictures—small in size and painted, as it were, *against* the grain of Piper's war work as an artist employed variously by the War Office, the Ministry of Information, and the organisers of the Recording Britain scheme—represent, with their engaged warmth, their richness of colour and texture, and their evident control, a substantial advance on the semi-abstract set pieces done at Stourhead and Holkham in 1940. Splendid as those largely conceived paintings are in their decorative effect, and in their noble scale, they lack the immediacy and the authority of these much smaller and much more intense communications.

There is a parallel advance in Piper's unofficial gouaches in these years: the somewhat tentative and deliberately dry tone of the Hafod drawings of 1939 goes, and there is an increasing certainty and assurance in the whole body of work making up the series of descriptive drawings done for the King at Windsor, and for Sir Osbert Sitwell at Renishaw, both of which were begun in 1941. Piper's association with Sir Osbert was a particularly happy one, and its harmony gave rise to what can now be seen to be a classic of English theatre design in the form of the front cloth for the 1942 production of the Sitwell–Walton *Façade*, an impressively "right" piece of work which is second only to his design for the fifth of the Walton–Ashton ballets *Quest* in its claim to be the most distinguished thing of the kind done in England in the decade. In both cases the designs are entirely responsive to the terms of the artist's commission, and at the same time sufficiently Piper's own in their strength and originality to establish an indelible impression on the mind's eye Once seen they are not readily to be forgotten, and they cannot be recalled without pleasure.

Piper turned another corner in his professional development in the year of the *Façade* design, achieving a very remarkable success in the art of book illustration. Asked, in effect, to decorate an anthology of descriptive verse chosen by John Betjeman and Geoffrey Taylor for publication under the title of *English, Scottish, and Welsh Landscape*, in W. J. Turner's and Sheila Shannon's New Excursions into English Poetry, Piper produced a series of lithographs and a cover design so powerful in themselves, and so beautifully in scale with the format of the volume, as to make the very ordinary commercial production (issued by Adprint under Frederick Muller's colophon) into one of the memorable books of the period. It is a measure of Piper's developing mastery of his technique that this book builds up a suggestion of rich colouring by its brilliantly controlled use of three of the anti-colours—black, Payne's grey, and yellow ochre. The book's plates, and those illustrating Park Place, Talland Church, and Stonesfield, in particular, are tours de force in which Piper exploits to its furthest limit every possibility open to him in the given context of a wartime commercial publication.

Such feats are not to be brought off in any happy-go-lucky spirit of having a go with what comes to hand, and it was noticeable at the time that Piper's always orderly workroom was being transformed into the scene of a skilled craftsman's exercise of his speciality. Everything in it that was for use was laid out with foresight and precision, and with an austere elegance, so that it fairly radiated the sense that its occupant was on top of his job. It was characteristic of the painter, too, that the efficient organisation of his workplace was matched, from the time of his stylistic breakthrough in the early 1940s, by its aesthetic quality. The personal environment he thereafter inhabited was as pleasing to look at as it was convenient. Up until that time he had been surrounded by the components of the bohemian style of the day.

The front room at Fawley Bottom, with its "found objects" in the way of flints and sea-worked stones anticipating the work of Arp and Henry Moore, examples of the work of vernacular artists without art—from hatchment painters to designers of eighteenth-century tobacco labels—and cottage china, could have been inhabited by any one of a great many of the like-minded people more and less in the modern movement with whom he had been on easy and friendly terms since his St Peter's Square days. The studio room was now dominated by things, images, and colours that were less eclectic and more personal, reflections of his own experience, needs, and interests, and no longer claims to belong. By the end of the 1940s Piper's workplace had become one in which it is inconceivable that any other work than his own could have been produced. He had, further, outgrown the front room of the farmhouse, and had moved into the large studio behind it which he had made out of a range of converted flint and brick farm buildings.

The beginnings of the personal maturation, of which this move was an indication, received official recognition when Piper was made a Trustee of the Tate Gallery in 1944. But he gave convincing demonstration of his new powers, and of his confidence in them, that made such official gestures unnecessary. He launched out on a period of brilliant creativity with his stage designs for Olivier's *Oedipus Rex* and Britten's *Rape of Lucretia* and *Albert Herring*, and with the beginnings of two impressively beautiful series of works done in Romney Marsh and Snowdonia. The Romney Marsh watercolour and mixed media drawings, sunlit, happy, *to p. 128*

120

79a

79b

79c

The Quest, 1943
79a   Design for scene V
79b   Sketch for scene I
79c   Design for scene II

80   *Job*, sketch, 1948

81 *Oedipus Rex*, sketch, 1945

82 *The Rape of Lucretia*, sketch, 1947

83 *Gloriana*, street scene (production photo), 1953

84 *The Turn of the Screw*, sketch, 1954

85

86

Dancing, 1952
85 Production photo
86 Sketch

Cranks, 1956
87 Production photo
88 Sketch for cloth

89 *Billy Budd*, model, below deck, 1951

Owen Wingrave, production photo, 1973
90 The Hall at Paramore

87 88

91 92

91, 92, 93 *A Midsummer Night's Dream*, three sketches, 1960

93

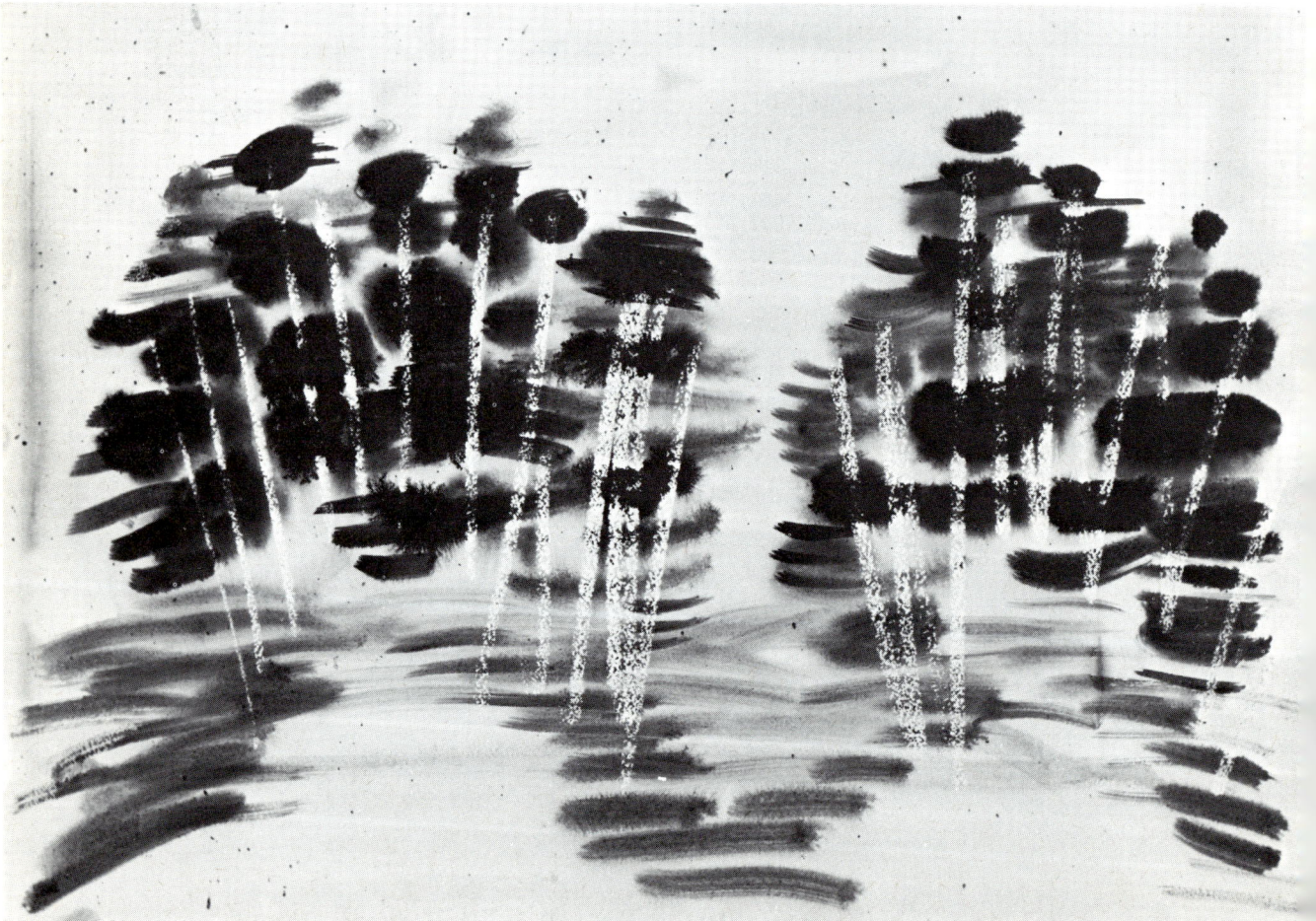

94 *A Midsummer Night's Dream*, production photo, 1960
95 *Death in Venice*, Arrival at the Lido, design for cloth, 1973

and lyrical in feeling, are in extraordinary contrast with the works in the Welsh series.

These, begun in 1947 when Piper acquired a cottage at Nant Ffrancon, became over the years the strongly expressed statement of a particular view of the natural order and the forces that shape the earth and hold the planets in their places. While re-thinking Turner during the later stages of the War, Piper had been reading Ruskin with rather more care and attention than his work usually gets, and had seen through his somewhat tendentious rhetoric to his discovery of geology as visible dramatic action expressing the tragedy implicit in the human condition as a creature aware of being a thing of the moment in an eternal universe. Piper's Welsh pictures from the Snowdon series are unique in English painting in their presentation of the continuing storm of creation, and in the intelligence of their interpretation of the facts of geology and landscape. They may also be said to be English painting at its finest in so far as they are entirely free of literature, conveying their message without even momentary resort to signs, metaphors, and symbols depending on arbitrary or customary associations of verbally formulated ideas. The statement made is expressed entirely in colour, and by the wonderfully firm and fluent handling of the material. The paint, and the painter's gesture, speak, and the effects achieved are as strong as they are beautiful.

Piper was well into this series, and had reached the height of his powers, in 1948, the first of fifteen splendidly productive years. The period began well with the magnificent Blake-inspired designs for the Vaughan Williams–de Valois ballet *Job*, and with the initiation of the new series of Portland drawings and paintings which was to be completed in the middle 1950s. These convincing performances were the prelude to greater achievements, of which the designs for the Glyndebourne *Don Giovanni* of 1949 and the Covent Garden *Billy Budd* of 1951, the lithographs done for Curt Valentin in Mourlot's studio in Paris, the Foliate Heads of 1953 (the germination of a seed planted by Cave's book on medieval roof bosses, of 1948), the Venice drawings and paintings of 1958–9, and the Roman series of 1960–2, are the characteristic examples.

But while involved in these sufficiently impressive exercises of his gifts Piper was also engaged on two other major projects with related subject matter, an enormous body of work constituting an encyclopaedic account of, in one case, English and, in the other, French monumental architecture. The drawings and paintings making up these two immense *to p. 147*

96 Second studio with first stained-glass panel done for J.P. by Patrick Reyntiens from a gouache and initials by a sign-writer discovered in Ireland (about 1951). (See also fig 99.)

97 J.P. with Patrick Reyntiens working on the cartoons for Liverpool Cathedral in the big studio, 1966

98 With Suzannah. Mural, "The Englishman's Castle," for the 1951 Exibition, in progress on the outside of the big barn (not then converted)

99 J.P. with Osbert Lancaster, Joy Mills and M.P. working on the models for Battersea Pleasure Gardens. One of Ursula Earle's cane figures on the right, 1950 or 51

100 Tapestry for Chichester Cathedral laid out in the square at Felletin, near Aubusson, with members of the firm of Pinton Frères who wove it, 1962

101   Dungeness Beach, oil on board, 6 × 8 in, 1947

102   Anglesey wall (photo J.P.)

103   Ruins at Tomen y Mur, Ffestiniog, ink, chalk and watercolour, $16\frac{3}{4}$ × 20 in, 1943

105

104 Llyn du'r Arddu, ink, chalk and watercolour, 20 × 15½ in, 1949

105 Snowdon from the Glyders, sketchbook, 1948

106 Cwm Idwal, ink, chalk and watercolour, 22 × 28 in, 1949

106

109

110

107 Rocks, Capel Curig, ink and watercolour, 22 × 27 in, 1950

108 Rock, Cwm Tryfan, oil, 25 × 30 in, 1950

109 Rock, Cwm Tryfan (photo J.P.)

110 Rocks on the Glyders, oil on canvas, 20 × 29 in, 1950

111 Rocks and Carnedd Dafydd from Llyn Ogwen, ink, chalk and watercolour, 21 × 26 in, 1950

112 Glaciated Rocks, Nant Ffrancon, ink, chalk and water-colour, 15½ × 20 in, 1944

111

112

113

113 Waterfall, mid-Wales, oil on board, c. 1940
114 Weathercote Cave, oil on board, 1943
115 Weathercote Cave, oil, 1943
116 Pistyll Cain, ink, chalk and watercolour, 1940
117 Mawddwy Valley, ink, chalk and watercolour, 1940
118 Above Pistyll Rhaiadr, ink and watercolour,
1940
119 Easgill (photo J.P.), 1943
120 Pistyll Rhaiadr, ink and watercolour, 1940

114

115

116

117

118

119

120

121 Russell monument, Strensham, Worcestershire, oil on wood, 30 × 25 in, 1947

122 Redgrave, Suffolk, watercolour and collage, 21 × 26 in, 1946

123　Rycote Chapel, oil on board, 24 × 20 in, 1946 (cf fig 47)

124 Rock Avenue, Portland, chalk and watercolour, 14 × 19 in, 1954

125 Stone gate, Portland, oil on canvas, 28 × 36 in, 1950

126   The Needles, Isle of Wight (photos J.P.)

27   Niton, Isle of Wight, oil on canvas,
0 × 24 in, 1951

128   Rowlstone Tympanum with a Hanging
Lamp, watercolour and collage, 28 × 32 in, 1952

129

130

131

132

129, 130, 131, 132 Variations on ancient seals, oil on board, each 10 × 20 in, 1954

133 Variation: dancers by Poussin, oil on board, 6 × 8 in, 1952

134, 135 Two Variations: Poussin Bacchanale, oil on board, each 4¼ × 10 in, 1952

134

135

series are in both cases backed up by a superb photographic archive, and by a great many sketchbooks. These last contain large numbers of rapidly executed and beautifully laconic sketches which, with their verve and spontaneity, include some of Piper's finest light work: some of them are things that fully justify the use of the word masterly.

Of the sketchbooks as a whole it may be said that in addition to being in themselves things of delight, they are of very great interest for the light they throw on Piper's working methods. They contain, in the form of impressions of their motifs made on the spot, the germs of almost all the major works produced in these years. The notations made before the motif with pencil, pen, and washes picked out with colour accents, were worked up in repeated studio trials. Piper would make ten or fifteen full-sized versions of a given motif before finding an acceptable treatment. In some cases, in which the solutions of the special problems of colour equivalence or formal structure were especially evasive, the site would, after a lapse of time, be revisited, and further analytic studies made. These would then become the basis for a further development of the large-scale studio treatments of the motif. A visitor to Piper's studio at a time when a particular motif was engaging him might find a big oil version of the subject on his easel, a couple of oil versions leaning against the walls, and five or six of the more successful studio versions of the preliminary sketches pinned to boards placed about the room as objects for contemplation.

Certain motifs, and certain locations rich in them—such as Stowe in Buckinghamshire—reappear in the sketchbooks again and again. These recurrences not only show how much thought and meditation on the specific motif lies behind every one of Piper's major works, they also demonstrate the way in which the development of his technique has constantly freshened his eye and deepened his vision: he has returned to his favourite sites to make new discoveries in the light of the new directions that his work has taken. That the directions and discoveries are new is not always apparent to those more interested in the subject matter of painting than in painting itself.

The large part of the sketchbook material that is devoted to English monumental architecture has a very close relationship to the note-taking activities which have been part of Piper's work for the Architectural Guides, and is especially liable to misunderstanding from that point of view, as is the finished work in that region. For many people the essential Piper is a picture of a decaying church, abbey, or great country house foundering in the storm of the *Zeitgeist*, and a proportion, both of those who like this subject matter as of those who dislike it, do not look beyond it to see what is happening and what has been done on the canvas or paper. The sort of event that the characteristic Piper painting is essentially can be seen rather more easily in the French sketch material, and in the finished work derived from it. Piper did not get into French monumental architecture until relatively late in the day, his pre-War visits to France having been more directed to French painting than to experience of the country that produced it.

In the middle 1950s, after 1953, he was drawn into France by, among other things, an opportunity to design for stained glass. The English stained-glass revival of the nineteenth century had petered out into a predominantly Pre-Raphaelite conventionalism by the turn of the century, and this art form was, perversely, most alive in England in the 1950s where it was most conventional and academic—a number of its practitioners being able to function with a certain dash and style in the manner of the fourteenth and fifteenth centuries. To find first-class work done in anything approaching the contemporary spirit it was necessary to go to France and Northern Europe.

Piper began working in stained glass with Patrick Reyntiens in 1954, and was then looking back to Bourges and Chartres for example and stimulus, much as Rouault had done when working out his stained-glass-orientated colour vocabulary. Working in the actual medium with Reyntiens soon showed Piper that the time for being *moyennageux* had gone by, and by the time he was given the commission for the big baptistry window in Coventry Cathedral he was giving thoughtful attention to the modern stained glass in contemporary French churches, and to what was being done in Germany and Switzerland. The sketchbooks show that he was at the same time giving a great deal of attention to Romanesque and Gothic France, in the specific regions of the Charente, Dordogne, the Limousin and Touraine. The earliest of these French topographical drawings are very much in the vein of Piper's

140   Variation on Giorgione: The Tempest,
ink and watercolour, 16 × 16 in, 1951

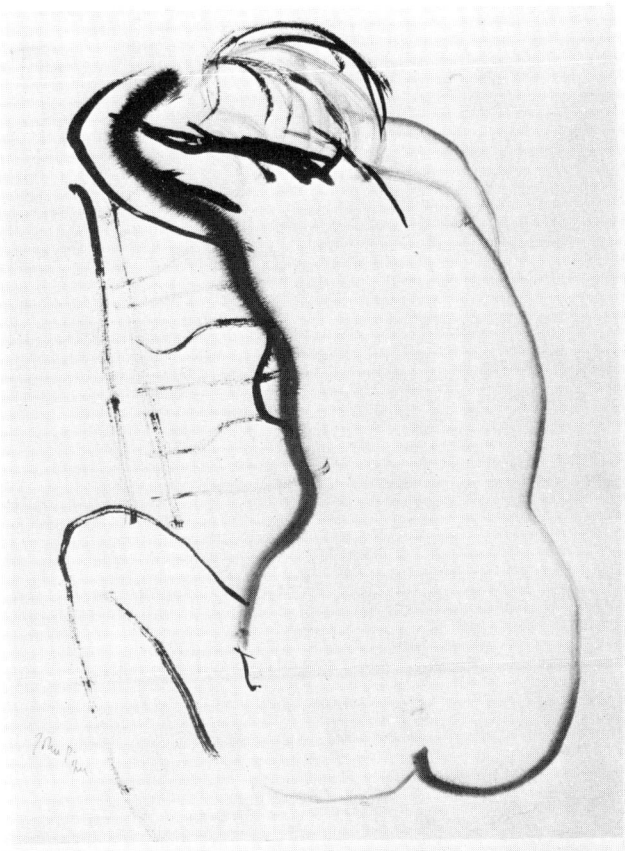

141   Life drawing, ink, 1952

142   Life drawing, ink and wash,
15 × 19½ in, 1953

143 Foliate Heads, chalk and watercolour, 1953

144a–d Foliate Heads, four chalk and watercolour drawings, each 21 × 27 in, 1953

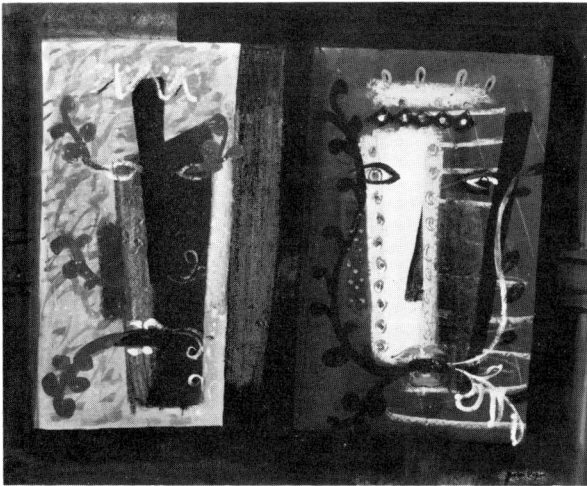

a

b

c

d

territory he has explored can be seen, in these illustrations, on the broadest basis.

He began in the later twenties acquiring composition; confining himself to abstracts and avoiding the distractions of atmosphere, personality, colour and light, at that particular stage. In the nineteen-thirties, he grasped problems of naturally observed textures and the 'atmosphere' of a place. Collage helped in this.

In the nineteen-forties he approached the business of 'subjects' and painted churches and beaches as 'semi-abstracts'. During the war, in the duties of Official War Artist he produced 'subject pictures' of churches and other features, in which the striking compositions were obviously the fruit of much contemplation and creation of abstracts, and in which the patterning of textures was closely related to those of the original subjects. Both the compositions and the textures were now being done with less deliberation; the processes involved had been absorbed and digested into the personality of the

artist and the execution of them, whilst based upon l[...] experience had become unconscious; flair replaced c[...]

His series of Welsh mountain landscapes in the [...] forties and early fifties took this a stage further; crys[...] lising his previous thirty years' study of composit[...] textures and the character and spirit of places. They [...] magnificent and represent a first flowering of [...] artist's maturity. Wilson would not have despised th[...] Constable would have unbent a little; Turner w[...] have been friendly, perhaps, and Ruskin enthusia[...] on seeing them.

Later in the forties he came to terms, tentatively, [...] the question of the human element; and in an expl[...] tory and compromise approach he peoples some st[...] of architecture with figures; but, like the architec[...] they are stone antiques; being tomb and mem[...] effigies. In 1952 his lifelong interest in archaeology [...] him to an unusual series of striking subject pictur[...] fonts, effigies, stained glass, tympana and so on; [...]

JOHN PIPER. *Monument, Boxted.* 1947. Water-colour and collage. 20×26 in. (Toledo, Ohio: Museum of Art)

JOHN PIPER. *Foliate heads.* 1953. Water-colour and chalk. 21×27 in. (Owned by the artist)

English work of the late 1940s and early 1950s, but as the baptistry window project drew to an end, and the painter moved on, in the direction of his wholly successful collaboration with Patrick Reyntiens on the glorious lantern for Liverpool (R.C.) Cathedral, the French and English landscape and architectural drawings and paintings undergo a series of subtle transformations.

The sketchbooks show that by using the transparent medium itself Piper came to much more than an appreciation of the colour range in which stained glass is outstandingly successful. He began to see colour itself in a new way, and entered a visual world of greater intensities and more lyrical feelings than had been within the realm of his previous experience. Though critics tend to ignore the point, there is nothing more stimulating to an artist than success, and Piper's knowledge that the Liverpool lantern had come off beyond his greatest expectations as one of the milestone achievements of modern English stained-glass design launched him on a second joyously creative period subtly different in character from that of 1948–63.

This new period is characterised by singing colour, boldly used. From its thrilling take-off in the lyrical Pembrokeshire, Scottish, and Macon landscapes of 1968 the work of the period climbed rapidly to the high points represented by the stunning French Gothic façades of 1970–1, the Chambord series of 1971, the Cardiganshire and Lac d'Annecy drawings and paintings of 1971–2, and the powerful and disturbing Connemara landscapes of 1972. One of the many factors that are at work in giving these masterly paintings their vitality and strength is the buoyancy of spirit that derived from Piper's knowledge that he had done very well indeed in his work with Reyntiens at Liverpool. The point is an apparently trivial one that may not be thought to throw much light on the question of Piper's painting, but confidence is, however subjective, a vital issue to a painter.

As it will have been seen, Piper's line of development from 1936 onwards had been against the grain of the general trend, and in his first post-War period he had been following a path very markedly his own. With Abstract-Expressionism, with the post-War Hard Edge abstractionists, and with the Episcope and graphics processmen who were coming up at the beginning of the 1960s, he had very little in common. His sense of isolation was much increased by a change of fashion in the theatre, a realm in which the new and fresh has a special value. In the 1950s the new had been sought by turning away from the professional stage designers and turning to artists. In the 1960s the

145 Stowe sketchbook, 1953

pendulum had swung the other way, and there had been something of a revolt against the concept of the picture-making approach to stage design.

Piper, who had been very much in, found himself chillingly very much out. For an artist the theatre is a bad place in which to be out, because there are few places less like an art gallery than a theatre—an institution which until recently has had a minimal loyalty to its own past. Scenery, costumes, and working drawings which have served their turn in the theatre are apt to be treated like so much rubbish, and it is bruising for an artist to find that almost every trace of his contribution to the dazzling success of five years back has since vanished.

But in the early 1960s Piper had more to contend with than the sense that some of his best work had been done on shifting sand. His

152

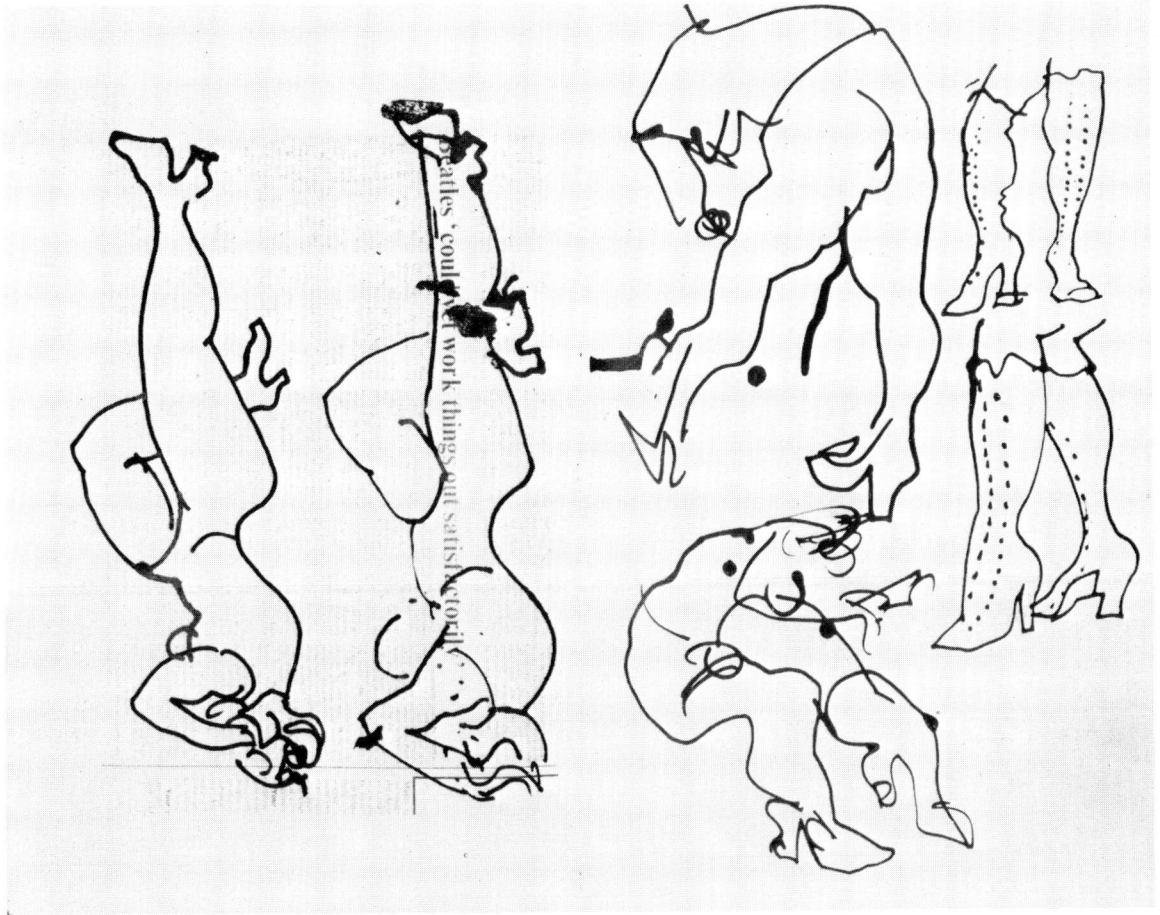

146 Sketchbook, 1971

appointment as a Trustee of the Tate Gallery of 1944 had been renewed when his first term came to an end in 1953 and he continued to serve on the board until 1961. There is nothing that can usefully be said about the troubles that beset this gallery towards the end of Piper's Trusteeship, they constitute one of those subjects which become the harder to understand the more one learns of them. All that is to the purpose is the very sad fact that the troubles centered on a personal matter, one of those gut hatreds of one man for another that breeds an infinity of malice and can last for a lifetime. Piper, an innocent bystander who was only marginally involved, by virtue of his office was taken by one party to be a partisan of the other, and as such made the target of a sustained campaign of derision and denigration intended to put an end to his professional career and to break his belief in himself.

That such things can be done, and that people can put time and energy into doing harm for harm's sake, may be hard to believe, but anybody who is in doubt as to the nature of the pressures that Piper was called on to withstand in these years should turn to the venomous attack upon him that *The Times Literary Supplement* saw fit to print as a purported review of S. John Woods' book of 1954 on his Paintings, Drawings, and Theatre Designs. The general direction of the campaign was to revive the old allegation that Piper was a defector from the Abstractionist camp who had never really understood what that movement was all about, that he had reverted to provincialism when England had been isolated from outside influences during the War, and that he had been peddling the mouldy fig of neo-Romanticism since its end. A major effort was put into making this the received view of Piper's career, and it was depressing for him to see that it gained ground in some quarters, leading, for instance, to his exclusion from the British exhibits at the Venice Biennale. An Arts Council publication of 1962 typically described the spirit behind his breakthrough into full maturity in the late 1940s and 1950s as "a nostalgic retreat into insular sensibilities".

But the lift to Piper's self-confidence provided by the Liverpool lantern releasing him from the dispiriting effects of this campaign was only a part of the story. One of the problems that Piper had faced as a stained-glass designer had been that created for all workers in this medium by the disintegration of the classic mediaeval stained-glass vocabulary by the enlargement of the available colour range consequent to the application of new chemical discoveries to the art of colouring glass. It was the need to create a valid personal discipline that would stand up in the face of the temptations of a release from all traditional restraints that led Piper to undertake a substantial rethinking of all his most cherished ideas about colour between 1953 and 1963. That the sufficiently impressive baptistry window at Coventry is to some extent a less convincing work than the Liverpool lantern reflects the fact that it reached the stage of commitment at an earlier stage in this rethinking process. The lyrical spirit, and the force, of the paintings of the years after 1968 is rooted in their status as its natural conclusion.

Working in stained glass Piper was continually faced with the problems of handling transparent colour masses, almost the antithesis of the painter's normal business with opaque reflecting surfaces. Contemplating his transparent medium Piper came at the end of the 1960s to perceive a new way in which he could boot the technique of oil-painting. He had played about with transparencies of the eighteenth-century and

154

147 Detail of mediaeval stained glass at Wilton (photo J.P.)
148 Tête de Jeune Fille, aquatint by Picasso, 1947
Illustrated together in *Stained Glass: Art or Anti-Art* by John Piper (Studio Vista, 1968)

early nineteenth-century varieties in the 1930s, painting on glass and oiled papers, but he now went very seriously after the use of colour oppositions and the inherent qualities of paint as the means of expressing the discoveries about colour that he had made while handling glass. He was trembling on the brink of success in the group of loosely painted landscapes done in the Dordogne, and the Bordelaise in 1967, but a lingering uncertainty expressed in an unhappy colour range running from brown through burnt orange to yellow and green, combined with a certain heaviness of brush stroke denied him what he was looking for. The effects of transparency, of the infinite visible through the accidents of surface incident, evaded him until he was painting in Pembrokeshire and Sutherland in the following year.

The breakthrough was achieved by following up the suggestions inherent in Dufy's work, with its characteristic use of calligraphy over colour masses, to draw a surface through which brilliant colour might be seen to pass. The strategy was made to work by purifying and raising the level of the intensity of the colours in Piper's palette, and by a tremendous and startling increase in the certainty and dash of his attack. The groping brush strokes of 1967 suddenly gave way to rapid and assured handling of paint, and the drawing, with both line and colour, rose to a new level. It was characteristic of the painter that he had discovered the solution to his problem of finding a mode in which to express the discoveries about colour that he had made while handling the essentially rigid medium of glass in the fullest exploitation of the fluidity and fluency of oil paint. On the brink of his seventieth birthday Piper, having achieved a style that gave him the power to encompass the Classical aim of liberating the essential from the accidental, and of seeing the moment through the eyes of eternity, had once again established himself as a painter of abundant promise. His latest work is the continuation of a story which has always been one of expanding knowledge and deepening insight, and is, if anything, richer in possibilities than it has ever been.

FINIS

149 Back gardens, Pembroke, ink and watercolour, 1953

150 Ironbridge, ink, chalk and watercolour, 15 × 22 in, 1957

151 Meurville, near Troyes, chalk and watercolour, 15 × 22 in, 1957

152 French Village, chalk and watercolour,
15 × 22 in, 1957

153 Village, near Fontenay-le-Comte,
15 × 22 in, 1958

154 Petit Palais, Gironde
(photos J.P.), 1956–7

155 Blasimon, Gironde

156 Collonges, Tympanum, ink and watercolour, 15 × 22 in, 1958

157 Vézelay, Tympanum, gouache, 22 × 30½ in, 1967

158 Christ between St Peter and St Paul, chalk and gouache, 22 × 15 in, 1958

159 Autun, Ghislebertus' drapery, chalk and watercolour, 22 × 15 in, 1967

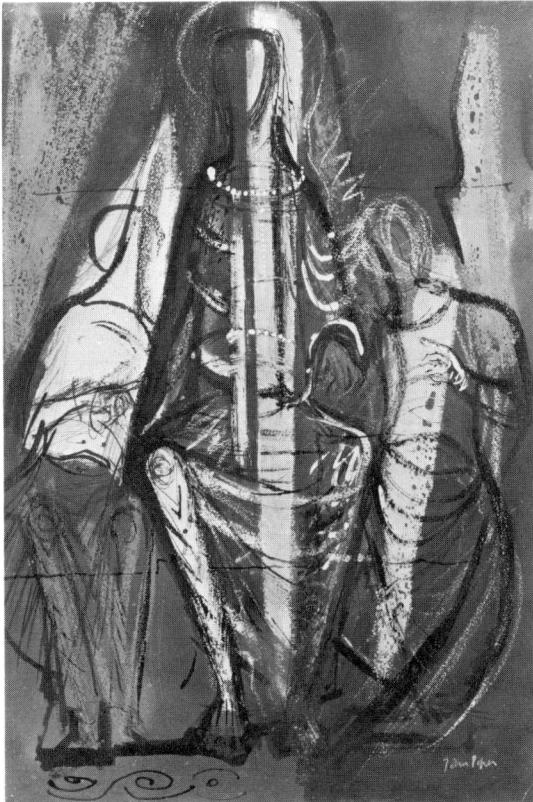

160 Three lancets, first study for Oundle Chapel east windows, ink, chalk and water-colour, 29 × 22 in, 1954

161 Sketch for Baptistry window, All Saints, Clifton. Executed in fibre glass

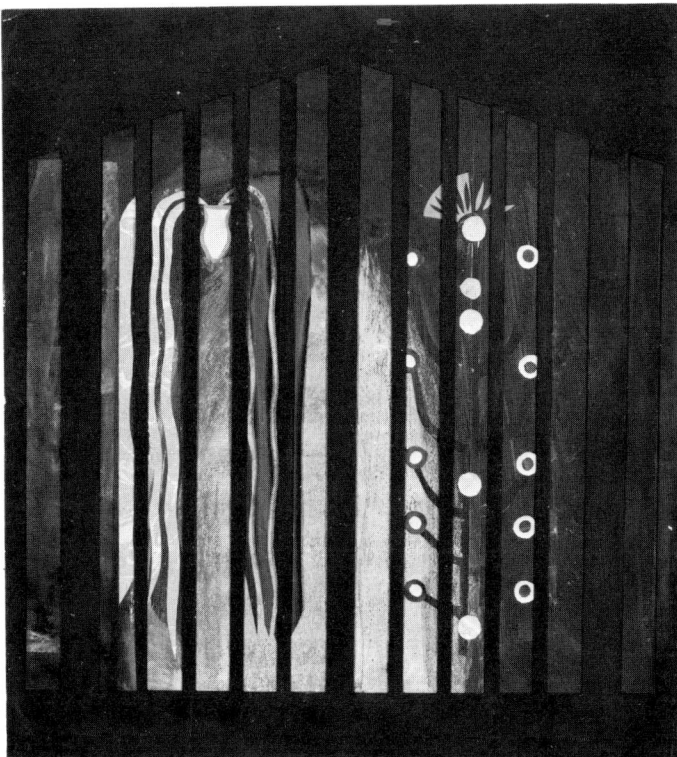

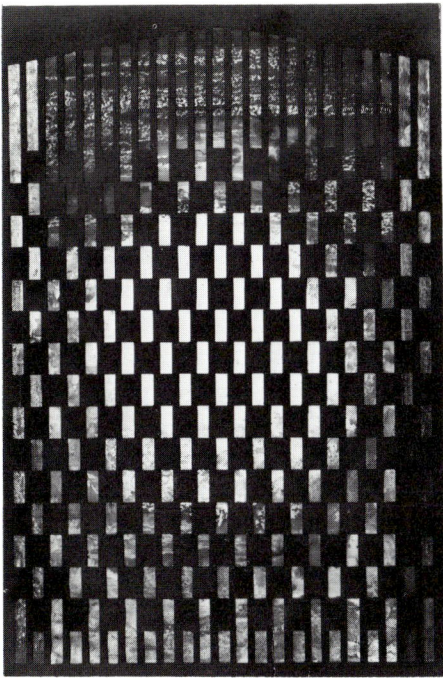

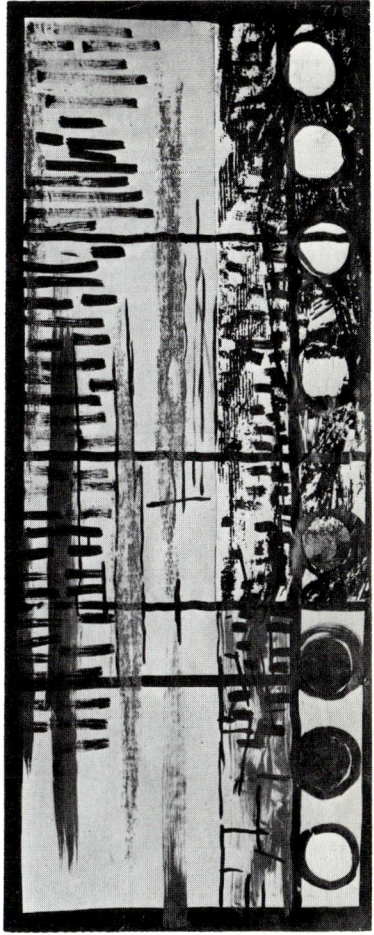

Baptistry window, Coventry Cathedral:
162 Cartoon for the working model,
1959

163a, b Two of the full-sized cartoons for
the panels, each 50 × 21 in, 1959–60

a

b

164 Sketch for the Liverpool Cathedral lantern (designed with Patrick Reyntiens)

165 Venice, the Piazzetta from the Clock Tower, oil, 44 × 34 in, 1959

166   Venice, the Salute from the Grand Canal below the Accademia Bridge, oil, 30 × 25 in, 1959

167

Venice

167 The Loggetta and the base of the Campanile, chalk and watercolour, 15 × 19 in, 1959

168a–d The Dogana from the Lagoon, sketchbook, 1959

169 The Salute and the Dogana, watercolour, 12 × 16 in, 1959

170 The Salute, oil on canvas, 48 × 60 in, 1960

171 St Mark's Square with the Loggetta and the base of the Campanile, oil on canvas, 28 × 36 in, 1960

172 Chiesa dell'Ospedaletto, watercolour, 15 × 11 in, 1959

173 Palazzo Rezzonico (photo J.P.)

168   **169**

170

171

172

173

174

174 Sheffield, oil, 36 × 48 in, c. 1960

175 Huddersfield, chalk and watercolour, 14 × 21 in, 1960

176 Sheffield, chalk and watercolour, 14 × 21 in, 1960

177 St Nicholas, Liverpool, lithograph, 1964

175

176

177

178

179

180

181

Entrance Gates

178 Fawley Court, ink and watercolour, 1940

179 Waddesdon, oil on board, 1958

180 Moonfleet, ink and water-colour, 1953

181 Malgwyn, Dyfed, ink, chalk and watercolour, 1970

182 Stone Hall, Welsh Hook, ink, chalk and watercolour, 16 × 22 in, 1952

182

185

183 Trajan's Column, water-colour, 1961

184 Colosseum, watercolour, 1961

183

184

185 Montepulciano, sketchbook, 1961

186 San Bonifacio, sketchbook, 1961

187 Ostia Antica, oil, 12 × 16 in, 1961

188 Soave (photo J.P.)

189

Brittany

189 St-Michel, watercolour, $13\frac{1}{2} \times 20\frac{1}{2}$ in, 1961

190 Pointe du Château, gouache and collage, 16×22 in, 1961

191 Poll Foen, gouache, $22\frac{1}{2} \times 31$ in, 1961

192 The Morbihan, gouache, $13\frac{1}{2} \times 20\frac{1}{2}$ in, 1961

190

191

192

193

Pembrokeshire

193 Bullslaughter Cliff, oil on hardboard, $9\frac{1}{2} \times 13$ in, 1962

194 Bullslaughter, White Caves, gouache and collage, $22\frac{1}{2} \times 30\frac{1}{2}$ in, 1962

195 Garn Fawr, oil on canvas, 23×42 in, 1962

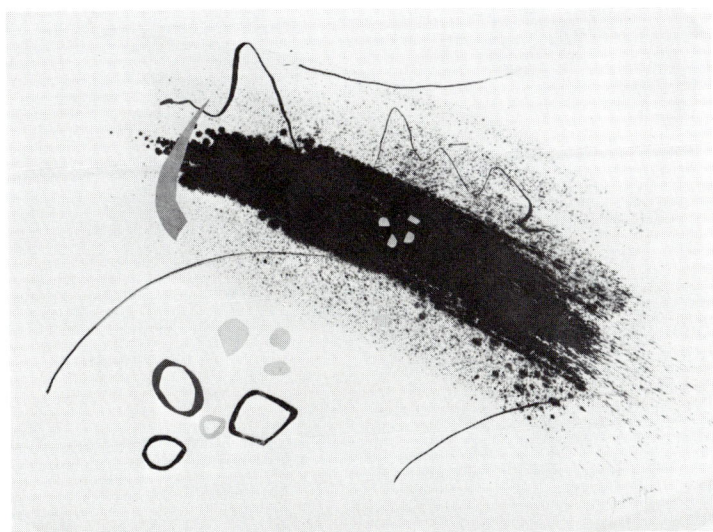

194

195

196 North Buckinghamshire Landscape, Waddesdon, watercolour, 1964

197 Hopfield, Ospringe, gouache, $15\frac{1}{2} \times 23$ in, 1968

198

199

200

198   Vale of Towy I, watercolour, $22\frac{1}{2} \times 31$ in, 1963

199   Vale of Towy II, watercolour, 1964

200   Devil's Bridge Waterfall,
gouache, $22 \times 15\frac{1}{4}$ in, 1968

201   Vale of Clywd, watercolour,
$15 \times 22\frac{1}{2}$ in, 1965

201

202

202   Parsac, near St-Emilion I, gouache, $14\frac{1}{2} \times 21\frac{1}{2}$ in, 1967

203   Carennac, Dordogne, gouache, 14×21 in, 1967

204   Parsac II, gouache, 22×30 in, 1967

205   Near Lochinver, Sutherland, gouache, $15\frac{1}{2} \times 22$ in, 1968

206   Mountain Landscape, Pembrokeshire I, gouache, 1968

203

204

207 Connemara, gouache, $15\frac{1}{2} \times 22$ in, 1969
208 Connemara, gouache, $23\frac{1}{4} \times 31\frac{1}{2}$ in, 1969

209 Kilmalkadan, Ireland, gouache, 32½ × 31 in, 1969

210 Quelven-en-Guern, Brittany (photo J.P.)

211 Killeshin, Ireland, gouache, $22\frac{1}{2} \times 31$ in, 1969

212 Le Martyre, Finistère, $14 \times 21\frac{1}{2}$ in, 1959

213 Haddiscoe, gouache, 23 × 15½ in, 1969

Dalham (Suffolk) 1-7/24/71   John Piper

214 Dalham, gouache, 23 × 15½ in, 1969

215 Harlaxton Manor, oil on canvas on board, 48 × 60 in, 1972
216 Chantilly, gouache, 15 × 21¾ in, 1971

217 Château de Maintenon, gouache, 15 × 23 in, 1973
218 Caernarvon Castle, gouache, 23 × 15½ in, 1969

219 The roof, Chambord, oil on
canvas, 60 × 70 in, 1964

220 Anet (photo J.P.)

221 Chambord (photo J.P.)
222 Chambord, gouache,
23 × 31 in, 1966

223 Addlethorpe (photo J.P.)

225 Avy, Charente, gouache, 31 × 22½ in, 1970

224 Terrington St Clement's, gouache, 22½ × 31½ in, 1975

John Piper

226 Le Mans Cathedral (photo J.P.)

227

228

227 La Trinité, Vendôme, oil on canvas, 60 × 42 in, 1969–70

228 Rheims Cathedral (photo J.P.)

229 Le Mans, sketchbook

229

230

231

232

233

234

Variations

230　Patinir, ink, 15 × 21¾ in,
1969

231　Benozzo Gozzoli, ink,
15 × 21½ in, 1969

232　Richard Wilson, Wilton
from the South East, gouache,
15 × 22¼ in, 1969

233　Richard Wilson, The Dee
near Eaton Hall, gouache,
15 × 22½ in, 1969

234　Gainsborough, gouache,
15 × 22 in, 1969

235　The Grand Vista, Belœil,
Belgium I, gouache, 9 × 21 in,
1968

236　The Grand Vista, Belœil II,
gouache, 6½ × 20½ in, 1968

237, 238　Etaing, near Arras I
and II, both 7½ × 21 in, 1968

235

236

237

238

COLOUR PLATES

Pl 1 Forms on Dark Blue, oil on canvas, 62 × 76 in, 1936

Pl 2   Autumn at Stourhead, oil on linen, 25 × 30 in, 1939

Pl 3   Seaton Delaval, oil, 28 × 36 in, 1942

John Piper

Pl 5 Notre-Dame-de L'Épine, Marne, oil on canvas, 60 × 42 in, 1971

Pl 4 Corton, Suffolk, oil on canvas, 79 × 39½ in, 1968–9

Pl 6 Pembrokeshire plough oil on canvas, 34 × 44 in, 1977

Pl 7   Buckden in a storm, oil on canvas, 34 × 44 in, 1977

Pl 8 Congreve Monument and Shell Grotto, Stowe, gouache, $22\frac{5}{8} \times 31$ in, 1974

Pl 9 Bridge and Boycott Pavilion, Stowe, gouache, $22\frac{5}{8} \times 31$ in, 1974

Pl 10   Connemara Landscape, oil on canvas, 48 × 60 in, 1972

Pl 11   Field Walls, Connemara, oil on canvas, $24\frac{1}{2}$ × 30 in, 1972

Pl 12 San Moisë, Venice, oil on canvas, 60 × 42 in, 1971

Pl 13 Venice Fantasy. With grateful acknowledgments to Ruskin as soft-ground etcher and to Chris Prater as screen printer. Silkscreen, 48×72 in, 1974

Pl 14 Study for *Death in Venice*, gouache, $29\frac{5}{8} \times 45\frac{5}{8}$ in, 1974

Pl 15 Château de Chambord III, oil on canvas, 60 × 60 in, 1971

Pl 16   Echillais, Charente, gouache, 23 × 30 in, 1968

Pl 17   Chadennac, Charente, gouache, 23 × 30 in, 1967

Pl 18   Jazenne, Charente, gouache, 22½ × 30½ in, 1968

Pl 19   South Lopham Church,
gouache, 27¼ × 15½ in, 1973

20

21

22

23

Pl 20   Withy bed, Earl Stonham, gouache, $15\frac{3}{4} \times 23$ in, 1974

Pl 21   Garn Fawr, gouache, $14\frac{1}{2} \times 22\frac{1}{2}$ in, 1970

Pl 22   Pembrokeshire Landscape, gouache, $15\frac{1}{2} \times 22\frac{3}{4}$ in, 1970

Pl 23   St-Léger, Charente, gouache, $14\frac{1}{4} \times 21\frac{1}{4}$ in, 1967

24

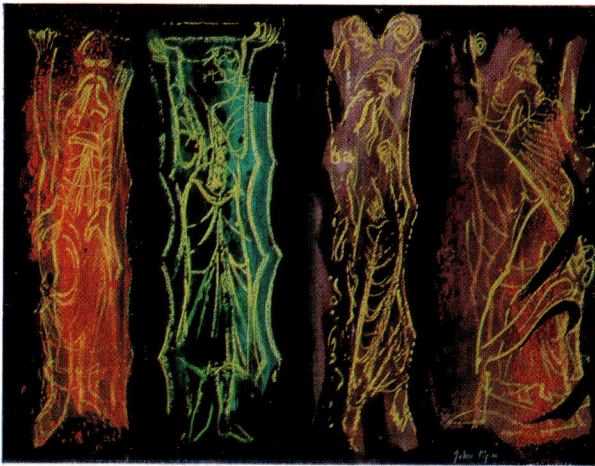

25

26

Pl 24 Cardiganshire hillside, oil on canvas, 34 × 44 in, 1970

Pl 25 Studies at Souillac, gouache, 22½ × 30 in, 1970

Pl 26 Flagellation: St-Gilles, Gard, gouache, 22½ × 30 in, 1971

Pl 27 Cley-next-the-Sea, gouache, 23 × 30½ in, 1973

27

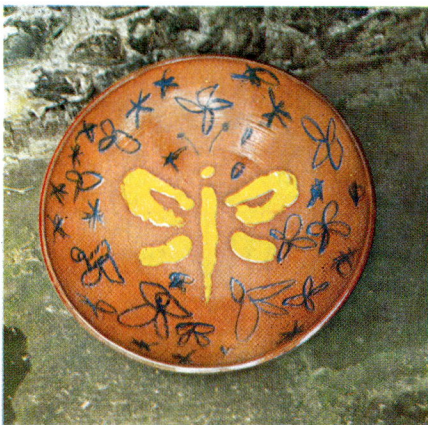

Pls 28–33 Ceramics, 1971

List of Illustrations

Appendixes on John Piper's Work

Books by and books illustrated by John Piper

Shell Guide to Oxfordshire (Batsford 1938; revised and re-illustrated Faber and Faber 1953)

Brighton Aquatints introduction by Lord Alfred Douglas (Duckworth 1939)

British Romantic Artists ("Britain in Pictures" series Collins 1942)

Buildings and Prospects (Architectural Press 1948)

Murray's Architectural Guide to Buckinghamshire with John Betjeman (John Murray 1948)

Murray's Architectural Guide to Berkshire with John Betjeman (John Murray 1949)

Romney Marsh (Penguin 1950)

Shell Guide to Shropshire with John Betjeman (Faber and Faber 1951)

Stained Glass—Art or Anti-Art (Studio Vista 1968)

English, Scottish and Welsh Landscape Verse chosen by John Betjeman and Geoffrey Taylor (Muller 1944)

Left Hand, Right Hand Sir Osbert Sitwell (Macmillan 1945)

The Scarlet Tree Sir Osbert Sitwell (Macmillan 1946)

Castles on the Ground J. M. Richards (Architectural Press 1946)

Great Morning Sir Osbert Sitwell (Macmillan 1948)

Laughter in the Next Room Sir Osbert Sitwell (Macmillan 1949)

On the Making of Gardens Sir George Sitwell (Dropmore Press 1949)

Wordsworth's Guide to the Lakes edited by Moelwyn Merchant (Hart-Davis 1952)

First and Last Loves John Betjeman (John Murray 1952)

Poems in the Porch John Betjeman (SPCK 1954)

The Natural History of Selbourne Gilbert White (Folio Society 1962)

India Love Poems translated by Tambimuttu (Paradine Press 1977)

Stage designs

Trial of a Judge 1937 Scenery and costumes
Group Theatre at Unity Theatre
Play by Stephen Spender Produced by Rupert Doone

Facade 1942 Front-of-stage cloth
Boosey & Hawkes at Æolian Hall
An Entertainment by Edith Sitwell and William Walton

The Quest 1943 Scenery and costumes
Sadlers Wells Ballet at New Theatre

Choreography by Frederick Ashton Music by William Walton

Oedipus Rex 1945 Scenery
Old Vic Theatre Company at New Theatre
Drama by Sophocles (tr. W. B. Yeats) Produced by Michel Saint-Denis

The Rape of Lucretia 1946 Scenery and costumes
Glyndebourne
Opera by Benjamin Britten Produced by Eric Crozier

Albert Herring 1947 Scenery and costumes
English Opera Group at Glyndebourne
Opera by Benjamin Britten   Produced by Frederick
 Ashton

Job 1948 Scenery and costumes
Sadlers Wells Ballet at Covent Garden
Choreography by Ninette de Valois   Music by
 Ralph Vaughan Williams

Simone Boccanegra 1948 Scenery (with John Moody)
Sadlers Wells Opera
Opera by Verdi   Produced by John Moody

Sea Change 1949 Scenery and costumes
Sadlers Wells Theatre Ballet
Ballet by John Cranko   Music by Sibelius

Harlequin in April 1951 Scenery and costumes
Sadlers Wells Theatre Ballet
Ballet by John Cranko   Music by Richard Arnell

Combattimento di Tancredi e Clorinda 1951 Scenery and
 costumes
English Opera Group at Lyric Theatre, Hammer-
 smith
Opera-ballet: Choreography by Walter Gore
 Music by Monteverdi

Don Giovanni 1951 Scenery and costumes
Glyndebourne Festival Opera
Opera by Mozart   Produced by Carl Ebert

Billy Budd 1951 Scenery and costumes
Covent Garden Opera
Opera by Benjamin Britten   Produced by Basil
 Coleman

Dancing 1952 Scenery and costumes
Kenton Theatre, Henley-on-Thames
Ballet by John Cranko   Music by George Shearing

The Shadow 1953 Scenery and costumes
Sadlers Wells Ballet at Covent Garden
Ballet by John Cranko   Music by Dohnanyi

Gloriana 1953 Scenery and costumes
Covent Garden Opera
Opera by Benjamin Britten   Produced by Basil
 Coleman

The Pearl Fishers 1953 Scenery
Sadlers Wells Opera

Opera by Bizet   Produced by Basil Coleman

The Turn of the Screw 1954 Scenery and costumes
English Opera Group at Venice Opera House,
 Venice
Opera by Benjamin Britten   Produced by Basil
 Coleman

The Prince of the Pagodas 1957 Scenery
Royal Ballet at Covent Garden
Ballet by John Cranko   Music by Benjamin
 Britten

Cranks 1956 Scenery
St Martin's Theatre
Written and devised by John Cranko   Music by
 John Addison

Less than Kind 1957 Scenery
Arts Theatre
Play by Derek Monsey   Produced by Yvonne
 Mitchell

Il Ballo delle Ingrate 1958 Scenery
Aldeburgh Festival
Opera by Monteverdi   Produced by John Cranko

Reflection 1958 Scenery
Edinburgh Ballet at Edinburgh Festival
Ballet by John Cranko

A Midsummer Night's Dream 1960 Scenery
English Opera Group at Aldeburgh
Opera by Benjamin Britten   Produced by John
 Cranko

Abelard and Heloise 1960 Scenery
Arts Theatre
Play by Ronald Duncan   Produced by Hugh Hunt

A Midsummer Night's Dream 1961 Scenery
English Opera Group at Covent Garden
Opera by Benjamin Britten   Produced by John
 Gielgud

Owen Wingrave 1972 Scenery
Covent Garden Opera
Opera by Benjamin Britten   Produced by Colin
 Graham

Death in Venice 1973 Scenery
English Opera Group at Aldeburgh Festival

Opera by Benjamin Britten   Produced by Colin Graham

What the Old Man does is always Right 1977 Scenery and masks

Fishguard Festival
Opera by Alun Hoddinott   Produced by John Moody

Public Collections (selected)

Aberdeen Art Gallery and Industrial Museum
Birmingham City Art Gallery
Bradford City Art Gallery
British Council
Contemporary Art Society
Coventry City Art Gallery
Eire National Collection
Ferens Art Gallery, Hull
Glasgow Art Gallery and Museum
Glynn Vivian Art Gallery & Museum, Swansea
Guildhall Art Gallery, London
Harrogate Public Library and Art Gallery
Institute of Arts, Detroit, USA
Leeds City Art Gallery and Temple Newsam House
Leamington Spa Art Gallery and Museum

Manchester City Art Galleries
Museum of Modern Art, New York, USA
National Gallery of Canada, Ottawa
Phillips Memorial Gallery, Washington DC, USA
Pilgrim Trust, USA
Reading Museum and Art Gallery
Rio de Janeiro, The British Embassy, Brazil
Rochdale Art Gallery
Sao Paolo Museum, Brazil
Scottish National Gallery of Modern Art, Edinburgh
Sheffield Graves Art Gallery
Southampton Art Gallery
Toledo Museum and Art Gallery, USA
Wakefield City Art Gallery

Commissions

1941   Paint Renishaw for Osbert Sitwell
1948   Decorations for British Embassy, Rio de Janeiro
1951   Mural, Festival of Britain (with Osbert Lancaster)
1954   Stained glass, Oundle School Chapel
1955   Mural, Mayo Clinic, Rochester, USA
1957   Stained glass, St Andrew's, Plymouth
1959   Mural, Morley College, London
       Stained glass, Eton College Chapel
       Stained glass, Coventry Cathedral Baptistry window
       Mosaic, St Paul's, Harlow New Town
       Mosaic, BBC TV Centre
1961   Mural, SS *Oriana*
       Stained glass, Sanderson and Sons
       Stained glass, Llandaff Cathedral
1962   Mural in fibre glass, North Thames Gas Board

Stained glass, Nuffield College Chapel, Oxford
1963   Stained glass, St Mark's, Sheffield
       Stained glass, St Woolo's, Newport
1965   Stained glass, St Mary's, Swansea
       Stained glass, Metropolitan Cathedral, Liverpool (with Patrick Reyntiens)
       Tapestry, Chichester Cathedral
1966   Stained glass, All Saints, Misleston
       Stained glass, St Peter's, Babraham
1967   Stained glass, All Saints, Clifton
       Stained glass, St Margaret's, Westminster
1968   Stained glass, St Paul's, Bledlow Ridge
       Stained glass, Christchurch Cathedral, New Zealand
       Stained glass, Bakers Company Hall, London
       Tapestry, Civic Centre, Newcastle
1969   Stained glass, George VI Memorial Chapel,

216

St George's Chapel, Windsor
Stained glass, St Bartholomew's, Southcote
Stained glass, St Paul's, Pishill
1970 Stained glass, Churchill College, Cambridge
Stained glass, St Giles', Tottenhoe
Tapestry, Grocers Company Hall, London
1973 Stained glass, St Andrew's, Wolverhampton
Tapestry, Rothschilds Bank, London
Tapestry, Witwatersrand University, South Africa
1974 Stained glass, Churchill Memorial Window, The Cathedral, Washington DC
1975 Tapestry, Reading Civic Centre

Ceramic, Royal Arms, Reading Civic Centre (with Geoffrey Eastop)
1976 Stained glass, Nettlebed Church
Tapestry, British Embassy, designed for Bangkok, diverted to Helsinki
1977 Stained glass, St Mary's, Fawley
Stained glass, Charing Cross Hospital Chapel
1978 Tapestry, Sussex University
In progress Stained glass, Robinson College Chapel, Cambridge
Stained glass, Benjamin Britten Memorial Window, Aldeburgh

Principal One-Man Exhibitions

1938 London Gallery, abstract paintings and collages
1940 Leicester Galleries, London, paintings and watercolours
1945 Leicester Galleries, The Sitwell Country
1946 Leicester Galleries, designs for *The Rape of Lucretia*
1948 Curt Valentin Gallery, New York
1950 Curt Valentin Gallery
1951 Leicester Galleries, Stones and Flowers
1953 Aldeburgh Festival and Arts Council Gallery, Cambridge Paintings 1932–52
1955 Curt Valentin Gallery
1956 Kunstzall Magdalene Sothmann, Amsterdam, drawings and watercolours
1957 Durlacher's, New York; Leicester Galleries
1959 Leicester Galleries
1960 Arthur Jeffress Gallery, London, paintings and watercolours of Venice; Durlacher's
1962 Arthur Jeffress Gallery, paintings and watercolours of Rome
1963 Marlborough New London Gallery, London
1964 Marlborough New London Gallery, Retrospective Exhibition
1967 Marlborough Fine Art, London, Retrospective Exhibition

1967–8 John Piper Retrospective, museums throughout Britain
1968 Cecil Higgins Art Gallery, City Museum Bradford, Retrospective Exhibition
1969 Marlborough New London Gallery, European Typography 1967–9; Bear Lane Gallery, Oxford
1970 Hammet Gallery, London, gouaches and watercolours; Derwent College, York University; Century Galleries, Sonning; Pieter Wenning Gallery, Johannesburg; Folkestone Adult Education Centre, Retrospective Exhibition
1972 Marlborough Fine Art
1973 Marjorie Parr Gallery, London; Compendium Galleries, Birmingham; Frank Gadsby Gallery, Leicester; Pieter Wenning Gallery
1975 Marlborough Fine Art; Bonython Art Gallery, Sydney; Selective Eye Gallery, Jersey; Marjorie Parr Gallery
1976 Gallery Kasahara, Japan
1977 Marlborough Fine Art
1978 University College, Cardiff; Aldeburgh Festival; Rye Art Gallery; St Edmund's Art Centre, Salisbury; Glynn Vivian Art Gallery and Museum, Swansea

Index

Italic numerals refer to pages on which illustrations appear. **Bold** numerals refer to illustration numbers in the unpaginated sections, and ***bold italic*** numerals to colour plate numbers.
Except where otherwise stated, all works indexed are by John Piper.